The church exists to make a desperately needed invit with urgent grace and eager hearts. Listen and need the sound of the trumpet.

JOHN ORTBERG, pastor and author

Helpful discipleship books are being published every month. But this one is different and rare. This book is linked with a very useful instrument that looks at your spiritual growth through the eyes of yourself and others—a 360-degree view. Defined qualities (eight) and characteristics (twenty-one) of discipleship are listed. Through this book and instrument, a person can begin to assess the strong and stunted areas and find joy in serving and in growth. The best chapter might be the one on how to coach someone through the discipleship process. Don't miss this one!

JIM SINGLETON, director of mentored ministry at Gordon-Conwell Theological Seminary

As a US denominational leader during a critical time for the church in this nation, Dana fully understands the strategic significance of discipleship for the credibility and authenticity of the movement that claims Jesus as Lord. He knows that the nondiscipleship of the church undermines everything we seek to do. We must correct this deficit or continue to decline. Pay attention!

ALAN HIRSCH, author of *The Forgotten Ways* and *5Q* and coauthor of *Untamed*

In *Simple Discipleship*, Dana Allin brings together two of my favorite topics: coaching and discipleship. His thesis in this book—that discipleship happens primarily through life experiences and relationship rather than listening to sermons and reading books—is absolutely right. He also gives the reader practical tracks to run on: specific qualities and characteristics of a disciple, tips for creating a personalized disciple-making plan, and a path to implementation. Dana is clearly writing from a wealth of experience, and our churches would all be stronger if we followed his lead.

BOB LOGAN, coauthor of *The Discipleship Difference* and *Becoming Barnabas*

If it bothers you that the church in North America is overprogrammed and underdiscipled, start reading this book today. Dana Allin delivers on a clear and compelling way forward in a tool that will invigorate and accelerate real disciple making in your church.

WILL MANCINI, founder of Auxano and coauthor of *God Dreams*

Discipleship continues to be one of the biggest challenges of the twenty-first-century church, both in the West and in the East. *Simple Discipleship* is a clear, passionate, and very practical account of who a disciple is and how to go about making one. It is a beautiful and timely gift to the church of the Master Disciple Maker.

REV. DR. MEHRDAD FATEHI, executive director of Pars Theological Centre

Christ's mandate to the church is this: Make disciples. Do you have a method? Dana distills years of Christian leadership into a simple process. This book is a gift to any who wish to live their lives in the likeness of Jesus Christ or help others do the same.

TIM MCCONNELL, lead pastor of First Presbyterian Church, Colorado Springs, Colorado

Grow Your Faith,

Transform Your Community

simple
discipleship

Dana Allin

A NavPress resource published in alliance
with Tyndale House Publishers, Inc.

NavPress is the publishing ministry of The Navigators, an international Christian organization and leader in personal spiritual development. NavPress is committed to helping people grow spiritually and enjoy lives of meaning and hope through personal and group resources that are biblically rooted, culturally relevant, and highly practical.

For more information, visit www.NavPress.com.

Simple Discipleship: Grow Your Faith, Transform Your Community

Copyright © 2018 by Dana Allin. All rights reserved.

A NavPress resource published in alliance with Tyndale House Publishers, Inc.

NAVPRESS is a registered trademark of NavPress, The Navigators, Colorado Springs, CO. The NAVPRESS logo is a trademark of NavPress, The Navigators. *TYNDALE* is a registered trademark of Tyndale House Publishers, Inc. Absence of ® in connection with marks of NavPress or other parties does not indicate an absence of registration of those marks.

The Team:
Don Pape, Publisher
David Zimmerman, Acquisitions Editor
Elizabeth Symm, Copy Editor

Cover design by Nicole Grimes.

Cover photograph of spheres copyright © by MirageC/Getty Images. All rights reserved.

Author photograph by Skye Coleman, copyright © 2018. All rights reserved.

Unless otherwise indicated, all Scripture quotations are taken from *The Holy Bible,* English Standard Version® (ESV®), copyright © 2001 by Crossway, a publishing ministry of Good News Publishers. Used by permission. All rights reserved. Scripture quotations marked NIV are taken from the Holy Bible, *New International Version,® NIV.®* Copyright © 1973, 1978, 1984, 2011 by Biblica, Inc.® Used by permission. All rights reserved worldwide.

Some of the anecdotal illustrations in this book are true to life and are included with the permission of the persons involved. All other illustrations are composites of real situations, and any resemblance to people living or dead is purely coincidental.

For information about special discounts for bulk purchases, please contact Tyndale House Publishers at csresponse@tyndale.com, or call 1-800-323-9400.

Cataloging-in-Publication Data is available.

ISBN 978-1-63146-713-4

Printed in the United States of America

24	23	22	21	20	19	18
7	6	5	4	3	2	1

To my wife, Beth, who is a constant example
of what it means to love and follow Jesus.
To my children, Micah, Peyton, and Piper,
who fill my life with joy. It is a privilege to be your
father and watch you grow in life and faith.

Contents

Foreword

THERE'S AN EXERCISE I LIKE to do early on with church teams
that have asked for help in building a disciple-making culture.
We apply the four quadrants of a SWOT analysis to answer the big
question "When it comes to discipleship in our church, what is
going well (**s**trengths)? Where is there frustration (**w**eaknesses)?
Where is there opportunity (**o**pportunities)? Where is there confu-
sion (**t**hreats)?"

It's fascinating how often the lack of a clear disciple-making
process appears in the "weaknesses" and "threats" categories.
Often, it's the pastor who makes that observation!

I suspect most of us realize the need for a clear, robust, flex-
ible, reproducible process for growing disciple-making disciples
of Jesus in our context. It is usually in the practical implementation, however, where systems break down.

Part of the problem begins with our misunderstanding of what
it means to be a disciple, and thus how we go about making them.

Discipleship is not primarily an exercise in information
transfer (although, of course, in our discipleship we are to use
our minds and intelligence to the utmost degree!). It is not a
syllabus to master but rather a friendship to experience more
deeply. When Paul says, "Be imitators of me, as I am of Christ"

(1 Corinthians 11:1), he reminds us that the biblical picture of discipleship is a journey far more than it is an event, and it requires other followers of Jesus around us, since the Christian faith is always lived out in community.

This is where the genius of Dana's book comes in.

Through the big idea of growing disciples in heart, head, and hands, we gain a framework for teasing out our thinking and practices. As he describes eight qualities and twenty-one supporting characteristics of a disciple—supported by a fabulous assessment tool—we are given clarity of language to review our personal (and our churches') disciple-making efforts.

There are so many helpful and practical ideas in this book. While it can't possibly answer every question (because it's your job to incarnate these ideas into your specific situation), Dana gives a robust set of tools to help you build a healthy process for making disciples who are growing and going with the gospel.

A hugely gifted, experienced pastor and pioneering national leader, Dana Allin brings an uncommon breadth of insight and understanding. He is a dynamic man of God who loves Jesus with abandon and passion—someone you want to follow into the mission field! I can unambiguously confirm that he lives this out personally: Recognizing that their first disciple-making focus is their children, Dana and his wife, Beth, are raising a family of world changers.

I'm privileged to speak and work with many national leaders, and Dana is the real deal. Please read and engage in this book, plundering the ideas and suggestions to strengthen and deepen your own—and your church's—disciple-making practices!

ALEX ABSALOM

cofounder of dandelionresourcing.com and churchinnovationlab.com

The Main Thing

"IF I AM HONEST, I'll admit that I don't really know how to make disciples." I remember when those words came out of my mouth. I had been in the pastorate for almost a decade, and despite sermons, programs, Bible studies, and small groups, many of the people I pastored weren't becoming more deeply devoted followers of Jesus Christ. For all of my effort, I wasn't able to make disciples—the primary task to which Jesus calls us!

There were some good things happening in the church, of course. Some people were growing, and others were coming to Jesus. For that, I was thankful. But the fruit seemed random and relatively disconnected from any strategic effort.

I was somewhat relieved when I read the book *Move: What 1,000 Churches Reveal about Spiritual Growth* by Greg L. Hawkins and Cally Parkinson. Churches that had much larger budgets and staff than mine, and preachers who were more eloquent than myself, also seemed to be treading water in the area of discipleship. It gave me comfort that I was not the only one facing this challenge. However, relief quickly turned to sadness: The church in the United States was, by and large, missing the mark.

Today, leaders are less afraid than they were back then to admit that their churches are not doing a great job of making disciples. Leaders don't necessarily post to Facebook or tweet the sentiment. But leaders of congregations of various shapes, sizes, and denominations express disappointment over the quantity and quality of disciples being developed in the ministry.

We all know that the core task of our congregations is to make disciples. We all know the great commission in the end of Matthew 28 is to "go therefore and make disciples of all nations," and we know that making disciples means to teach people to "observe all that [Jesus has] commanded." We indicate this sentiment in mission statements such as "To make disciples who make disciples" or "To know Christ and make Him known" or "To love God, love others and make disciples." There is no lack of knowledge or agreement that our core task as individuals and as a church is to make disciples. So why aren't we doing it? Why aren't we fulfilling the main task of the church?

ASSEMBLY-LINE DISCIPLESHIP

One of the greatest inventions in manufacturing was the establishment of the assembly line. This ingenious approach allowed a person on an assembly line to have one job that they repeated thousands of times a day rather than many jobs that they repeated less frequently to achieve the same end: a finished product. The line was filled with hundreds of people with individual jobs. Products could be made quickly and consistently every time.

In the name of making disciples efficiently, we have adopted an assembly-line mind-set to create disciples in our church. We have made assumptions, probably without a lot of thought, about how to adopt speed and efficiency into our disciple-making process, with the anticipated outcome of mass production. We assume that, like building a car, making disciples is a linear process. For example, we expect that weekend worship can produce many disciples.

However, if we stop and reflect on our own development as disciples, we will probably find that our growth didn't come from an assembly-line process. Usually, our growth has come through a combination of personal time with the Lord and interactions with mentors and other disciples, experiences and opportunities that stretched us and caused us to grow. We may have been particularly touched by a few sermons, but they weren't the primary factor in our growth as disciples.

JESUS KEPT IT SIMPLE

When Jesus made disciples, He used some simple principles to develop the people around Him. These principles and processes were so simple that they could be used with people of any educational level or socioeconomic class, from highly educated religious leaders like the Pharisees (John 3) to a man who had just been healed from a thousand demons (Mark 5). These principles were then repeated from generation to generation. What developed was a movement of faithful and mature followers of Jesus.

While Jesus didn't outright list these principles for making disciples, they can be deduced as we observe His interactions and see these patterns repeated in the interactions of Jesus' followers. We even see these principles being utilized all over the world in places where there is exponential growth in the quality and quantity of disciples.

And yet, in the modern Western world, we don't see much of a movement. We have a lot of what would be considered advantages for discipleship: freedom to assemble as large groups in worship, access to information that increases in volume more rapidly than we comprehend, seminaries and educational institutions, and a growing number of organizations that offer a plethora of discipleship books, curricula, and programs. These are wonderful privileges, and they absolutely have their place. I wonder, however, if at times this richness of resources has actually muddied the waters of discipleship. Do we sometimes miss the ultimate purpose of the great commission: helping people become more in love with Jesus and more reflective of His character in the world? Have we made discipleship more complicated than it needs to be?

A SIMPLE PROCESS

The first section of this book is a high-level view of the nature of being a disciple. We will examine the great commandment—the love of God with head, heart, and hands, with a corresponding love of neighbors—to consider what, at the fundamental level, characterizes a disciple. We will then look at the foundational approach of Jesus toward His disciples. This examination will help contrast Jesus' approach with the way in which we consider discipleship in our congregations.

The second section of the book takes a deeper look at what it looks like to follow Jesus as someone who loves God with head, heart, and hands. We have identified eight qualities and twenty-one supporting characteristics of a disciple. These have been mined from Scripture and articulated with the help of a variety of experts in the field; they will help disciples consider their personal spiritual health as followers of Jesus. An accompanying simple discipleship assessment will help us get feedback from people in our lives. This invaluable tool will encourage us to see ways in which we have matured and help us uncover areas where we might give more concentrated effort. The result will set the stage for a personal plan for discipleship. (There is more information about the simple discipleship assessment in appendix A. You can also find a code printed on the inside cover of this book that will allow you to take the assessment for free.)

The third section of the book will help you design a personalized process through which you can grow in specific areas of discipleship. As this plan develops, it will include personalized activities for engaging with God and others. This practical and experiential plan will encourage growth in knowledge of the truth. As these elements come together, they will foster personal maturity.

The fourth and final section will help leaders within the congregation incorporate simple discipleship principles into the larger structure of the congregation. Congregations may want to implement simple discipleship into small groups or a Sunday school program, in missional communities, or in one-on-one discipleship. This section will help a congregation create an environment conducive to multiplying disciples.

Incorporating what is presented in *Simple Discipleship* can be both easy and difficult in your church context. On the one hand, *Simple Discipleship* doesn't require you to change your structure, spend a lot of money, or hire additional staff. *Simple Discipleship* will, however, be challenging, in that structures will likely change and leaders will need to rethink their assumptions in light of this new emphasis on making disciples.

My experience has been that incorporating this type of simple discipleship into the church is a welcome addition. Lay leaders are hungry for a simplified approach to disciple making, one that retains a robust vision for mature disciples. We all want to understand what a disciple is, to know where God is calling us to grow, and to flourish in our personal discipleship. If we can clear the clutter from our vision for discipleship, we will see disciples growing in number and maturity in our congregations, our ministries, and our communities.

CHAPTER 1

The Essence of a Disciple

JULIA WAS COMPLETING her last quarter of seminary and applying to different pastoral positions within her denomination when she received a call to a small congregation only an hour away from her school. She was thrilled to begin pastoring this congregation that was just shy of a hundred members and averaged about seventy people on a Sunday. This was an older congregation, and Julia saw lots of potential to reach its surrounding neighborhood.

Shortly after she got to the church, the church council discussed what should be her most important priorities. Four of the six elders expressed the need for the church to reach younger families; they were glad that Julia and her husband were at the church. But then a member of the church council timidly raised his hand. "What good," he said, voice trembling, "is a full church when nobody is growing? We need to focus on helping people become disciples of Jesus first—then we can figure out how to bring more people in."

This man's statement caused a robust—and, at times, heated—discussion. Some members argued that the church was great at making disciples. Look at how many of their members had been at the church thirty years! Surely these were great models of what a disciple was. Other members challenged this assertion: Yes, the church had many members with longevity, but were these members really growing as disciples?

As the meeting progressed, Julia reflected on her seminary experience and realized that she never gained a clear understanding of what a disciple was, let alone how to develop one. The meeting ended with the council concluding that one of the next steps would be to develop a working definition of a disciple—including some characteristics that they hoped would be produced in a disciple through the ministry of the church.

One of the biggest challenges associated with developing a culture of discipleship is a lack of a clear, mutually-agreed-upon understanding of a disciple of Jesus. When a church doesn't have a unified vision around the characteristics and nature of a disciple, it will likely have a challenge making disciples. As is often said, if you aim at nothing, you will hit it every time. A church can have a mission statement centered around making disciples, but if the nature of discipleship is unclear or there are competing visions of what it means to be a disciple, the church will never fulfill its mission.

At the foundation of this book are eight core qualities and twenty-one subordinate characteristics of a disciple. These qualities and characteristics will be further unpacked and given biblical support in chapters 3 through 7, but for now, we will take a thirty-thousand-foot view of what it means to be a disciple of Jesus. Our definition is based first and foremost upon the great commandment found in Matthew 22:34-40.

> *But when the Pharisees heard that he had silenced the Sadducees, they gathered together. And one of them, a lawyer, asked him a question to test him. "Teacher, which is the great commandment in the Law?" And he said to him, "You shall love the Lord your God with all your heart and with all your soul and with all your mind. This is the great and first commandment. And a second is like it: You shall love your neighbor as yourself. On these two commandments depend all the Law and the Prophets."*

Just prior to this passage, the Sadducees, a group of Jewish leaders who didn't believe in resurrection, tried to give Jesus a problematic scenario to prove that there is no resurrection. Jesus, as always, gave a response that they didn't expect, and they went away speechless. It is then the Pharisees' turn to try to trip up Jesus. They want to see Him diminish aspects of the law by lifting up one part of the law over the others. So, in a patronizing tone, they ask Jesus to name the greatest commandment.

Jesus' response is again unexpected. He answers the

question not by lifting up one of the Ten Commandments found in Exodus 20 or Deuteronomy 5; instead, He elevates what is known as *the Shema*, which means "hear" in Hebrew.[1] It is found in Deuteronomy 6:4-5: "Hear, O Israel: The LORD our God, the LORD is one. You shall love the LORD your God with all your heart and with all your soul and with all your might."[2]

To this general command, He adds a second part to the command from Leviticus 19:18, indicating that we are to love our neighbors as ourselves. Then He says, "On these two commandments depend all the Law and the Prophets." Some translations, like the NIV, use the word *hang* rather than *depend*, which underscores that these two commandments are like a skeleton: Other commandments and prophetic statements from the Scriptures become the flesh. Jesus is not elevating one commandment over the others; rather, He calls these commandments the greatest because they encompass God's call on our lives.

If we test Jesus' statement, we find it to be true, of course. We can't break any of the other commandments and still have kept the great commandment from Matthew 22. If we love God with our whole selves, then we will worship Him alone, we will honor His name, and we will keep the Sabbath. If we love our neighbors as ourselves, we will not commit adultery, we will not lie, we will not steal, and so on.

If all of God's desires for our lives can be summed up by the great commandments, then perhaps this verse is foundational to our understanding of discipleship. In this command, Jesus lifts up three aspects of ourselves with which we are to love God. We are to love Him with

- our whole hearts;
- our whole minds (or, as this book will say, "head"); and
- our whole might (this book will use "hands," that is to say, our actions).

LOVING GOD WITH OUR WHOLE HEARTS

The Greek word for "heart" is *kardia*.[3] From this word, we derive many medical terms, such as *cardiologist*; however, just as we use the word *heart* to convey something more than just the muscle that pumps blood through our body, so the Jews and the Greeks had deeper meanings as well. The heart is symbolic for several aspects of our lives.

The heart can symbolize our inner passions, desires, affections, and longings. An example of this use of the term *heart* is when Jesus tells us in Matthew 6:19-24, "Lay up for yourselves treasures in heaven." In verse 21, He says, "Where your treasure is, there your heart will be also."

The heart can also be symbolic for our interior lives with God and our closeness to Him. In Matthew 15:8-9, Jesus quotes Isaiah 29:13, saying,

This people honors me with their lips,
    but their heart is far from me;
in vain do they worship me,
    teaching as doctrines the commandments of men.

Jesus and Isaiah are illustrating that some people were good at appearing to be close to God. In reality, however, external facades masked a disconnect between the people and God.

A final usage of the word *heart* is to describe one's character and integrity. In Mark 7, Jesus has been having heated interactions with the Pharisees over the nature and importance of their cleanliness rules. Jesus' accusation is that the Pharisees are elevating their own traditions above the commandments of God. He goes on to say that having clean hands does not actually make a person clean; we are not made unclean by things outside our bodies—rather, our impurity comes from within. Jesus makes His point in Mark 7:21-23:

> *For from within, out of the heart of man, come evil thoughts, sexual immorality, theft, murder, adultery, coveting, wickedness, deceit, sensuality, envy, slander, pride, foolishness. All these evil things come from within, and they defile a person.*

Notice that this list of sins includes both items that are visible and items that are invisible to the outside world. The external, visible sins are things like theft, murder, and slander. The internal sins, which may not be visible to others, are things like pride, coveting, and evil thoughts. When we were developing the simple discipleship assessment and engaging in the validity studies, some of the individuals taking the assessment realized that they didn't have people in their lives who knew them deeply enough to answer these questions. Some of these participants had been in small groups for years and yet still didn't have people who really knew them. Because some of these matters of the heart can easily be hidden from others, it is important that we develop relationships where people know us intimately and have access to see the things that might be hidden from our normal sphere of connectedness.

Three of the eight core qualities we identify in *Simple Discipleship* pertain to matters of the heart. These qualities are discussed at length in chapters 3 and 4.

LOVING GOD WITH OUR WHOLE MINDS

The second aspect to the great commandment is that we are to love God with our whole minds. There is a little bit of a change in the way Jesus quotes the Shema in Matthew 22:37. In Deuteronomy 6:5, Moses uses the wording *heart, soul,* and *might*, but in Matthew 22:37, Jesus says *heart, soul,* and *mind*. The challenge in interpretation is that *might* and *mind* are two very different concepts: *Mind* has to do with our intellect, and *might* pertains to our physical nature.

The reason for the apparent discrepancy in the parts with which we are to love God is that the word *soul* can also have a variety of nuanced meanings. Over the centuries, the particular aspects of *soul* that have been emphasized are varied. In the Hebrew understanding, which is the understanding present in the Shema, the aspect of *soul* that was emphasized was what we would normally classify as the characteristics of the mind. In the Greek understanding of the word *soul*, the emphasis was placed more on physical acts of doing, where we are to love God with our actions—or, as we will say throughout the book, "qualities of the hand." So in essence, in the Shema, Moses is saying that we are to love God with our hearts, minds, and actions, and in Matthew 22:37, Jesus is saying to love God with our hearts, actions, and minds. For the

7

purposes of this book, we will focus on the concept of loving God with our minds.

The ability to engage our minds in our love for God is a wonderful gift. The Lord has given us His Word not only as a means of connecting with Him but also to learn who God is and identify His purposes in the world. We learn who He has created us to be and what our mission is. In Romans 12:2, Paul tells us that the way in which our whole selves are to be transformed is by the renewing of our minds. As we engage our minds and let His Word and truth saturate our thought processes, we will be transformed individuals for the Lord.

Many times in Scripture, the Lord calls His people to have a better understanding of His Word and to pass on the truth of His Word to others. Perhaps one of the best passages to illustrate the expectation that God has for us to grow in our understanding of God's Word is Hebrews 5:11-14. The author of Hebrews writes in the previous verses about how Jesus is from the priestly order of Melchizedek. Then he stops, almost midthought. It is as if he realizes that by continuing on this line of thinking and giving his explanation, he would just cause greater misunderstanding among the people, because they didn't have the capacity to understand. The author writes,

> About this we have much to say, and it is hard to explain, since you have become dull of hearing. For though by this time you ought to be teachers, you need someone to teach you again the basic principles of the oracles of God. You need milk, not solid food, for everyone who lives on milk is unskilled in the word of righteousness, since he is a child.

But solid food is for the mature, for those who have their powers of discernment trained by constant practice to distinguish good from evil.

In this passage, there is clearly the understanding that God expects our minds to grow. He has the expectation that we grow in our knowledge of His Word, that we grow in our ability to process deeper theological truths, and even that we all have the ability to teach other people. He uses the analogy of a move from milk (the basic doctrines of the Word of God) to solid food (deeper theological truths). What a great analogy that we can easily understand. We all know that babies need milk and they are unable to chew or swallow solid food.

I think of the growth of my own son, when he needed only milk or formula for the first couple of months. Then, after a few months, we would put a little bit of the first stage of rice food in his bottle with a bigger nipple. A few months later, he was eating pureed baby food that he could mush around in his mouth and swallow. The next thing I know, I am enjoying a rib-eye steak with my twelve-year-old son. Now, my son still enjoys milk—it helps the meatier food go down more easily, and he likes the taste—but people would look at him (and us) funny if he was still bottle-fed. And yet we don't bat an eye when people in our churches are only able to take in the basic elements of God after being Christians for more than a decade.

Core quality 4 examines the characteristic of the mind, our ability to know the Scriptures, and our capacity to continue engaging in His Word. These aspects will be fleshed out more completely in chapter 5.

LOVING GOD WITH OUR WHOLE MIGHT

One of the first sermons I ever preached was on serving God. A lady came up to me after the sermon and said, "That was a great sermon. I want to start serving God when I retire in ten years." God's Word, however, is abundantly clear: We are all to engage in His mission and purpose in the world.

Christianity is not a spectator sport. I heard it said once that oftentimes, life in the church is like a professional football game: thousands of people in the stands who desperately need exercise and a few people on the field who desperately need rest. Somehow, the church in the West has decided that participating in the work of God in the world is only for people with extra time on their hands.

There are two ways we engage in God's mission in the world. First, there are some things that we are called to do regardless of the specific gifts and callings that God has given us. For example, all of us are called to care for orphans (James 1:27), feed the poor (Matthew 25:35), and make disciples (Matthew 28:19).

The second way we are called to serve is by using our individual gifts to fulfill the specific ministries that God assigns us. One of those passages is 1 Corinthians 12, which gives some examples of the types of gifts that God has given to believers for building up the church. Paul's point is that all of these gifts must work together in order to fulfill God's purposes—no gifts or roles are more important than others. Ephesians 4 discusses the unity of the body and the different roles that are present within it: apostle, prophet, evangelist, shepherd, and teacher. Paul then says that the only way the whole body of Christ, the church, will be healthy and fulfilling its purpose is if each part of the body is functioning properly.

The final four qualities in the discipleship profile are related to loving God with our strength or actions. Quality 5 is related to our ability to take the posture and attitude of Jesus as we engage in the contexts where God has placed us. Quality 6 looks at our ability to engage others in discipleship, which includes sharing our faith with nonbelievers and then helping other believers grow into maturity. Quality 7 looks at our ability to commit to the Christian community, by being devoted to the mission of a congregation and having a closer community of believers who help one another grow. Finally, quality 8 is related to understanding and living out the specific ministries that God assigns us. These four qualities of a disciple are articulated more completely in chapters 6 and 7.

DISCIPLESHIP OUT OF BALANCE

It is easy for a disciple to be out of balance in these three general areas of discipleship—loving God with our whole hearts, minds, and might. Every believer will more naturally gravitate toward certain discipleship qualities and characteristics that align with his or her spiritual gifts. Particular churches and denominations will tend to emphasize one or two of these areas over others. It is important, therefore, to examine our personal discipleship to see if we are in balance. It is also helpful to examine our churches' approaches to discipleship for the same reason.

If a church emphasizes helping disciples love God with their hearts and minds but negates loving God with their hands, the church will become doctrinally pure and have a robust devotional life but will likely be insulated from the outside world. In this situation, individuals might selfishly think that the church exists to meet their spiritual needs and not focus on God's mission in the world. An example of this attitude might be the church at Laodicea in Revelation 3:14-22. Jesus says He knows their deeds, and they are neither hot or cold. This refers to the two streams of water that went into Laodicea: one from Colossae that was cold and refreshing and one from Hierapolis that was hot and healing. They both served purposes, but by the time those waters came to Laodicea, they were lukewarm and gritty; people would drink that water and immediately spit it out.[4]

If a church emphasizes loving God with the heart and strength but minimizes loving God with their minds, then the church will be passionate and action oriented but might not focus on making new disciples. In this scenario, the church might become more like a humanitarian organization that seeks to do good in the world. An example might be the church at Thyatira in Revelation 2:18-29: They are affirmed for their good deeds, and yet their theology is off. They tolerate false teaching to accommodate the larger community.

If a church emphasizes helping disciples love God with their heads and hands but minimizes loving God with their hearts, then the church might begin to function out of obligation and duty rather than joy. In these situations, a church can become very concerned about correct theology and getting people saved but fail to move people into a loving relationship with the Lord. An example of this scenario might be the church at Ephesus in Revelation 2:1-7. This church had great theology—they could test those who claimed to be apostles and find them doctrinally false. They were doing good things in the community, and the society was changing. Yet Jesus said that they had lost their first love. They lost their loving relationship with God. They were functioning purely out of duty and not out of being joyfully connected to the Lord.

It is crucial for a church to have a clear picture of what it means to be a disciple of Jesus Christ. If the fundamental purpose of the church is to develop disciples, then an understanding of what it means to be a disciple is crucial. This book suggests that disciples are, at the root, those who love God with their heads (minds), hearts (souls), and hands (actions). In the next chapter, we will look at the way Jesus developed disciples.

REFLECTION QUESTIONS

1. Of the three overarching ways we love God, which do you most naturally gravitate toward? Head—loving God with our minds? Heart—loving God with our passion and character? Hands—loving God with our actions? Explain.

2. Looking at the same three areas, which might you shy away from? Why?

3. Who do you know that is a good example of living out all three areas well? Where do you see them living them out?

4. Where does your church or small group tend to put more focus? Where do they focus less?

5. Who are three to seven people that you could ask to take the discipleship assessment on your behalf?

$*$ $\underline{3}$

Chapter 2 & 3

Jesus—the
Great Disciple Maker

PASTOR BILL WAS FRUSTRATED. After ten years as the pastor of his church, he was not sure his church was making disciples. The most frustrating part was that several years ago, Bill and his elders had recognized their need to be more intentional about making disciples. Bill preached several ten- to twelve-week sermon series around their mission, "Making Disciples Who Make Disciples." During those sermon series, all of the Sunday-school classes and small groups used their time to reflect on the previous Sunday's sermon. Bill dedicated portions of elder meetings to teach discipleship and even began to pair up older, more mature disciples to meet with younger disciples and new believers. Bill complained to other pastors in his covenant group, "I feel like our church has learned a lot about what it means to be a disciple. But I am not sure they have actually become better disciples."

Bill's sentiments resonate with many pastors who passionately want those in their churches to grow as disciples. They spend a lot of time discussing the concept of discipleship and yet often do not see a great increase in the quality of discipleship in their churches.

Jesus not only gives us instructions about the nature of discipleship but demonstrates principles about how disciples are developed. This chapter will look at seven principles that Jesus consistently used as He developed the people around Him.

PRINCIPLE #1: Jesus Focused Efforts Where His Disciples Needed to Grow

The story of the rich young ruler (Luke 18:18-30) is a great example of this principle of discipleship. This young man who is described as a ruler is of a Jewish background and appears to have plenty of zeal for his Jewish faith. He somehow recognizes the uniqueness of Jesus and approaches Him with a humble posture. He asks, "Good Teacher, what must I do to inherit eternal life?"

Jesus responds by listing off five of the six commandments that have to do with our relationships with other people. Jesus says, "You know the commandments: 'Do not commit adultery, Do not murder, Do not steal, Do not bear false witness, Honor your father and mother" (verse 20).

The man responds that he has done all of these things since his youth. Presumably, he thinks that Jesus is going to congratulate him on a job well done and say, "Welcome to the club!"

But Jesus doesn't do that. Instead, Jesus shows His ability to know the true heart of a man and what a man is still missing. Jesus says, "One thing you still lack. Sell all that you have and distribute to the poor, and you will have treasure in heaven; and come, follow me" (verse 22). When Jesus initially listed five of the final six commandments to the young man, He did not mention "Do not covet." This is the exact commandment that was lacking in the life of the rich young ruler. Jesus must have known that if He simply listed the commandment about coveting earlier, the man would have assumed that he had not broken this commandment. After all, he wouldn't need to covet—he was already rich!

In a sense, the fundamental discipleship issue keeping this man from the Kingdom was the fact that he was coveting his own material possessions. Jesus exposed the ruler's weakness as a disciple by asking the question differently and challenging him to sell all he had and give to the poor. You can likely think of other passages where Jesus helps a person discover the profound heart issue that is hindering that person from a deeper relationship with Christ. Jesus exposes the real issue despite an individual's exterior facade of righteousness.

Jesus' methodology is very different from the approach to disciple making that is often taken in North American churches. In the name of efficiency or unity, we approach people's discipleship programmatically or corporately: All people, we tend to assume, need to grow in the same area. For example, what if Jesus challenged the rich young ruler with a lesson about not having sex outside marriage? This isn't a bad lesson—in fact, it is a lesson that many other people need to hear and respond to. But it wasn't the area in which the rich young ruler needed work. In fact, if Jesus had focused on cautioning the young man against premarital sex, it would have led the young man to continue believing that he was perfect.

Like Pastor Bill, we might often run a small group through a study or small-group curriculum. Sometimes we will have church-wide studies that go along with a sermon series. These are obviously not bad things to do in the life of a church. Many times, these studies can be helpful and unifying for the body. But they do not often lead to widespread obedience to and discipleship of Jesus, because they do not address where a particular person needs to grow in their own discipleship.

Jesus, being omniscient, has the advantage of knowing exactly where each disciple is strong and weak in their personal discipleship. For us mortals, identifying the area where you or someone you are working with needs to grow as a disciple can be challenging. The simple discipleship assessment can therefore be a valuable tool to discern relative areas of health and potential places for growth as a disciple.

PRINCIPLE #2: Jesus Ensured Growth Was Connected to Being Gospel Centered

The second aspect to a healthy approach to discipleship is ensuring that it is gospel centered. A gospel-centered approach is one that anchors any plan or motivation for spiritual growth to the joy people find in their identity in Christ. This probably seems self-evident; however, it is very common to unintentionally root discipleship in guilt or obligation. Sometimes those who disciple others imply that we are saved by grace but grow as disciples by a lot of hard work and discipline.

There certainly are passages in Scripture that lead us toward the idea that discipleship takes a level of discipline. For example, in 1 Corinthians 9:26-27, Paul says, "I do not run aimlessly; I do not box as one beating the air. But I discipline my body and keep it under control, lest after preaching to others I myself should be disqualified." So while it does take work to grow, sometimes the way this growth is portrayed to disciples is that this effort comes purely through one's own power.

The truth is, however, that we are not only saved by grace but we continue to grow as disciples through the grace and power of the Holy Spirit working within us. Galatians 5:22-23 does not list love, joy, peace, and so forth as the fruit of very hard work. These are instead the fruit of the Spirit, the characteristics that are produced in us as we let the Spirit of God work in our lives. This is fantastic news that not only is our salvation due to God's grace but our growth as believers is also a result of God's grace.

There are two opposite approaches to motivating people to grow that are *not* gospel centered. The first is to motivate people to grow out of guilt or shame. We don't see Jesus motivating out of guilt, but rather out of love. The perfect example is Jesus' interaction with the woman caught in adultery (John 8:1-11). The first thing that Jesus does for her is to extend His forgiveness and grace. In fact, in extending His forgiveness and humiliating the Pharisees, He is effectively signing His own death warrant. The extent of the sacrificial love and mercy that are given to this woman would be very evident to her. It is only *after* Jesus gives her His love and mercy that she is called to "go, and . . . sin no more" (verse 11). Her call to sin no more is not a way to prove that she is worthy of God's love; rather, it is to be a transformational response to God's love for her. Having a gospel-centered approach to discipleship means that we seek to help people desire to grow as disciples of Jesus because of His love for us.

Scripture is full of the understanding that the motivation and power to grow as disciples are rooted in God's love and grace toward us. In John 15, when Jesus talks about abiding in Him and the pruning that must take place to bear fruit, He prefaces these words by reminding the disciples that they are already made clean in Him (verse 3). In Romans 2:4, Paul says, "Or do you presume on the riches of his kindness and forbearance and patience, not knowing that God's kindness is meant to lead you to repentance?" Paul also tells us that the good works that we are to do in the name of Jesus (Ephesians 2:10) come after our understanding that it is by grace that we are saved by faith, and salvation is not based on works (Ephesians 2:8-9).

The other way that people are sometimes falsely motivated to grow as disciples is by thinking they are somehow earning extra credit. It used to be more widely said of such people that they were doing good works to earn more "jewels on their crowns in heaven." It is as if victims of this false motivation know that salvation is based on grace but think that heaven involves competing for the best status.

In our practice of discipleship, it is tempting to feel either like we are earning greater favor with God when we succeed or like we lose some of God's love when we fail. If we can understand that our position in Christ never changes despite our perceived success or failure, we will approach our discipleship from a much healthier perspective.

PRINCIPLE #3: Jesus Engaged in "Just-in-Time" Training

Just-in-time training is giving people information or a skill when they are in the best position to learn it. Ideally, this will be when they can immediately apply the information or skill. This is different from how we normally approach training in church. We might say that normally we practice *just-in-case training*. We tend to give people all the information they could potentially need just in case the worst scenario happens. The challenge is that people don't often retain information or skills when they are not in a position to utilize them.

In Luke 11:1, Jesus has just finished praying. The content of Jesus' prayer is unknown, but it is obvious that the disciples were with Him when He prayed. The assumption is that Jesus' prayer was powerful, because after His prayer one of the disciples asks Him, "Lord, teach us to pray." In response, Jesus teaches the disciples the Lord's Prayer. This prayer is given as an actual prayer to pray, but it is also a great model for the elements that should be contained in prayer. Jesus then goes on to teach the disciples about persevering in prayer by giving them the hypothetical situation of a friend that knocks in the middle of the night needing bread. In this story, Jesus indicates that even sinners are still willing to give good things, even if only to get rid of a late-night visitor. Jesus then tells them, "If you then, who are evil, know how to give good gifts . . . how much more will the heavenly Father give the Holy Spirit to those who ask him!" (verse 13).

These are extremely important lessons about prayer that the disciples needed to learn. And yet Jesus doesn't share these lessons until well into His journey with them. Why did Jesus wait so long? Probably because the disciples were not ready to receive those lessons. If Jesus had given them the same lesson previously, perhaps His words would have gone in one ear and out the other.

We see plenty of other examples of Jesus' timely teaching of the disciples. In Mark 9, the disciples are perplexed about why they cannot cast out a particular demon. Jesus takes the opportunity to give them brief instruction about prayer. The disciples would not have been prepared to receive this instruction if they had not just experienced a ministry failure and been trying to understand what went wrong.

Another way just-in-time training works is training people and then offering them the opportunity to use that training. Neil Cole, author of many books, was teaching a class in my doctoral program, and he said that one of the things he does with young protégés is train them to preach. He said something fascinating that made a lot of sense: "I don't train people to preach and then find an opportunity for them to preach. I find them an opportunity to preach, and then I train them. They are much more motivated to learn to preach once they know they are going to have to preach."

PRINCIPLE #4: Jesus Gave
People Opportunity to Reflect after Acting

Several times in the Scriptures, Jesus sends out the disciples to engage in ministry tasks and allows them to reflect on their experience afterward. In Luke 10:1-12, Jesus commissions the seventy-two, instructing them on how to engage in the work of the Kingdom. Jesus not only sends them out but also gives them the opportunity to reflect on their experience.

In verse 17, the group comes back and says, "Lord, even the demons are subject to us in your name!" Now this should have been information that they already know from watching Jesus and from the instructions that He gave. However, they learn this information in a deeper way through experience, and they are able to reflect on that experience with Jesus. It is then that Jesus gives them even more information about the fall of Satan, Jesus' authority over the enemy, and His protection of the disciples.

When things are delegated in the church, follow-up reflection is often overlooked. But follow-up is extremely important to maximize learning from a situation. The standard five-step process for helping people learn a new skill is

1. I do, you watch, we talk
2. I do, you help, we talk
3. You do, I help, we talk
4. You do, I watch, we talk
5. You do, someone else watches

This process helps ensure that people have adequate opportunity to reflect even before they are directly engaged with a ministry task and then continue to reflect as they assume various degrees of responsibility for a task. This process also helps ensure replication: The task of raising a new leader is not finished until a new apprentice has been identified and training has begun.

PRINCIPLE #5: Jesus Understood
Discipleship as More Than Simply Dispensing Information

Perhaps one of the biggest downfalls in many contemporary approaches to discipleship is thinking that the more information we have, the more transformation will occur. While information is certainly an important part of discipleship, information is only one of several aspects needed for life change. A phrase that I have heard and said frequently (though I am not sure of its origin) is that we are "educated way beyond our obedience." We have no shortage of information! We have a plethora of sermons, blogs, books, and articles, and most of them contain important and useful information. Our problem, however, is not information—it is action.

I doubt that there are many people in our churches who are unfamiliar with Jesus' commandment to love our neighbors as ourselves. When that commandment is preached about or read, there aren't a whole lot of people who walk away saying, "Wow . . . I have never heard that before!" When I preach about basic things like needing to read our Bibles and pray, I joke that it isn't rocket science. It isn't revolutionary new information. The challenge, however, is to *actually do what Jesus tells us to do*.

When we look at the way Jesus made disciples, He certainly

gave information. But true discipleship was about being transformed. In the previous chapter, we looked at the great commandment from Matthew 22, where we are to love God with our hearts, souls, and minds. The core concept here is that being a disciple of Jesus involves more than simply engaging the mind.

At the end of the Sermon on the Mount in Matthew 7:24-27, Jesus makes the comparison of two people who build their houses. One person is wise and builds their house on the rock, and one is foolish and builds their house on the sand. When the storms come, the house on the rock remains standing and the house on the sand falls. Jesus says that He is giving the analogy to compare two types of people. The person who builds on the rock is the person who hears the Word and applies it, and the one who builds on sand hears the Word of God and doesn't apply it. The application is clear: Simply having enough information isn't true discipleship—true discipleship involves application and transformation.

PRINCIPLE #6: Jesus Knew
Disciples Were Not Made at Microwave Speed

When I went to seminary at Fuller in Pasadena, I used to love to go to Baja Fresh whenever possible. Baja Fresh had a slogan on their wall that said, "Baja Fresh food cannot be made at microwave speed." This was stated to help customers realize that they may not deliver food as fast as traditional fast-food restaurants because it takes time to make the quality of food they produce.

Most approaches to discipleship assume that change

happens rapidly. Most of our church calendars assume that it happens in a week. Every week in worship, Sunday school, or small groups we have a new topic or passage to study that applies to our lives. The following week we move on to something else. But as we think about this strategy, we intuitively know that we can't have life transformation from a lesson and an application question.

If we have a nine-week study on the fruit of the Spirit, spending one week on each aspect, we expect to see significant transformation in that area. If we are really going to become more joyful, though, we are going to have to do several different types of activities and focus intensively on allowing the Spirit to produce joy in us over a longer course of time.

Jesus knew that developing disciples was time and labor intensive. He spent three years teaching and training His disciples intensively. He taught concepts to His disciples multiple times in a variety of ways in order for each one to truly be transformational. In chapter 8, we will look at how to design a growth plan that incorporates multiple activities to cultivate a particular aspect of discipleship.

PRINCIPLE #7: Jesus Asked More Questions Than He Gave Answers

In his book *The Questions of Jesus*, John Dear looked at all of the times that Jesus asked questions in order to draw people into a deeper understanding of Himself and discipleship.[1] His premise is that by asking questions rather than simply disseminating information, Jesus helped people grow more deeply.

This happened because being asked questions forced the disciples to think more critically about matters of faith rather than simply being given information. Questions help people stimulate their own thinking so that they are better able to process new information.

The other advantage of asking questions is that people are much more likely to follow through on commitments that they make as a result of being asked questions. I once counseled someone who continually needed to be in a relationship and wasn't happy or satisfied unless she had a boyfriend. She was continually discouraged by the quality of boyfriends and dates she would receive. I would continually encourage her to work on making herself a healthy disciple in order to be ready for a relationship, if that was God's intention for her life. After many long conversations about the same topic, we were getting nowhere. Eventually, I asked her what she thought she should do. After a few other questions, she finally came to the conclusion that she should work on herself and her relationship with the Lord before entering a dating relationship. I was certainly a little frustrated that I had said this many times previously with no positive result. But I learned a lesson that day: People are more likely to follow through on plans that they discover for themselves.

In chapter 9, we will want to consider that the person who is discipling someone else should really take the function of a coach. Yes, there will likely be some times when information or advice needs to be given. However, as we engage with other people in their discipleship, they will be better served if we approach our role as that of a coach, asking powerful questions and engaging in active listening.

These principles of Jesus seem so obvious, and yet it is probably not difficult to think of times when we or our churches have operated contrary to these principles. You may want to refer back to this chapter when you read chapters 8–10 of this book and begin developing your own plan for discipleship, helping others grow as disciples, and making a disciple-making culture. In order to do each of those things well, it will be continually important to incorporate these principles.

REFLECTION QUESTIONS

1. Think about times in your life when you have grown as a disciple. Which of the principles that Jesus used were active in your own transformation?

2. Which of these principles do you tend to use or see used in your church to help others grow?

3. Which of these seven principles of Jesus were new to you? Reflect on their importance in discipleship.

4. Why are these principles relatively obvious and yet so hard to apply? What works against the application of these principles?

5. How might you incorporate one or more of the above principles into relationships where you are helping others grow (in formal small groups, intentional discipling relationships, or the informal relationships you have with other Christians)?

CHAPTER 3

Gospel Identity

The Center of a Disciple

CHUCK WAS AN ELDER in his church. Now sixty years old, Chuck had grown up on a farm in Kansas. His parents were devout Christians who did as little work on Sunday as is possible on a farm. Sunday was dedicated to going to church in their Sunday best and eating an afternoon meal (prepared the day before) with their extended family. Chuck's parents abstained from smoking, drinking, and cursing. His mother and father gave time to their local church and would say to Chuck, "When we are at the pearly gates, we want to hear, 'Well done, good and faithful servant.'" When Chuck was disciplined as a child, his parents would say things to him like "No, Chuck, good Christian boys don't do that" or "Chuck, God is watching, and you don't want to disappoint Him, do you?"

When he grew up, Chuck followed the example of his parents. He volunteered and tithed and lived a morally virtuous life; however, Chuck was not experiencing much joy in his Christian life. He was often judgmental of others who were not living the way he thought they should. He complained to the pastor and other senior members of the church about the younger people and their lack of commitment and being so casual in their appearance on Sunday. If you asked Chuck his definition of a disciple, he would center that definition on a list of behavioral dos and don'ts. Chuck is a perfect example of the older brother in the story of the Prodigal Son.

THE LOST SONS

Jesus tells the story of a father with two sons. The younger son approaches the father and indicates that he wants the half of the inheritance that he will receive upon his father's death. The father grants the request, and the son proceeds to squander his inheritance in immoral living. This younger son realizes his sins and comes back to ask the father if he can be a servant in his household. Before the son can even get the words out of his mouth, the father greets him with open arms, dresses him in his finest robe, and begins to throw a party.

It is a great story of God's forgiving love that is bestowed upon us. But the story doesn't end with the restoration of the younger son. The father goes out to see his older son, who has refused to come in and join the party. The older son is livid that the father has lavished his brother with manifestations of his love while he has been doing everything the father has asked him to do and received nothing.

Christians like Chuck can often identify with the older brother. It doesn't seem fair that the older brother has done all of the right things and yet doesn't seem to have the same level of approval and acceptance as the younger brother, who really messed up and has not proven that he is a changed person.

At this point, it is helpful to ask, Who is really lost in this story? Most people will say that the younger son is the lost one. Certainly, the younger son was lost. This is fairly obvious; he separated himself from his father both physically and in his behavior. The reality, however, is that the older son is also lost. Presumably, he has been in his father's presence every day. He has been working hard for his father. He has, however, separated himself emotionally from his father's love. This older son thinks he should have earned his father's approval by this point. Look at his words in Luke 15:29: "Look, these many years I have served you, and I never disobeyed your command, yet you never gave me a young goat, that I might celebrate with my friends." The older brother is lost because he is taking his identity from his accomplishments and obedience rather than from his role as a son of the father.

Chuck might be prone to doing the same thing, as his identity is coming from what he has done for the church rather than from what God has done for him in Jesus Christ. The core issue for Chuck is that his identity and actions are not centered in the gospel. Chuck lacks joy because his identity is not gospel centered. Neither are his actions, which flow from his identity (Luke 6:45). He places unreasonable expectations on other people's expressions of faith and gives those expectations the weight of the gospel, when in fact, such expectations actually betray the gospel. Chuck is a disciple of a false gospel based on performance, and he is making disciples based on the same false gospel.

This might be a strange proposition. How could someone who has gone to church their whole life, who believes the central facts about the Christian faith, lives a morally correct life, and gives of their time and money to God's work at the church, not be centered in the gospel?

WHAT IS "GOSPEL CENTERED"?

Let us be reminded of the core of the Christian belief, that is, the Christian gospel. Then we can explore what it means to be centered in the gospel. Every other major religion has at its heart a fundamental belief that your spiritual reward or punishment is based upon what you do in your life. Karma, for example, is the idea that what goes around comes around. If you are a good person and do kind things to others, then the universe will reward you. If you are a bad person and are evil to others, then the universe will punish you. This idea is central to the Hindu religion, but many people have incorporated this life philosophy. You might recall the TV show *My Name Is Earl*. Earl had been mean and nasty to people in his life. He ended up winning the lottery, but his ticket was destroyed when it was run over by a car, and thus, he felt this was karma returning his evil upon him. Buddhists also believe that your actions in this life determine your spiritual reward or punishment. For the Buddhist, this belief is manifest in reincarnation, the idea that what you become in your next life depends on how well you do in your current life.

The Christian faith is entirely different. A Christian understanding is that you can never be good enough to earn a spiritual reward. In fact, if we received what we deserve, it would be death and spiritual separation from God for eternity. This biblical truth is reiterated many times throughout Scripture. For example, 1 John 1:8 says, "If we say we have no sin, we deceive ourselves, and the truth is not in us," and Romans 3:23 tells us "all have sinned and fall short of the glory of God."

Sin can be defined many ways, one of which is missing the mark of perfection set forth by Jesus Christ. This includes doing the things that God doesn't want us to do—obvious sins such as lying, stealing, and adultery, commonly known as sins of commission—but we can also commit sins of omission, not doing the good things that God calls us to do. The parable of the Good Samaritan (Luke 10) is a great example. The religious leaders who walked by the person who had been beaten, robbed, and left for dead didn't beat him personally, but they committed a sin of omission by ignoring his needs.

But there is another type of sin: the sin of an underlying attitude. As Jesus said in the Sermon on the Mount (Matthew 5), simply *not murdering* people isn't sufficient; we must seek to rid ourselves of underlying anger. It is not enough to simply abstain from committing adultery; looking at a woman lustfully is committing adultery in our hearts. Sometimes, our sins of attitude are when we do the right things with the wrong motivation. I have seen people who faithfully give 10 percent to the church, but their rationale is that if they give God 10 percent, then God will bless them tenfold. They might believe that

God will not allow them to experience hardship if they give faithfully. The individual is not really giving to God's work but rather approaching giving as either an investment or an insurance policy. When we start to see sin in its totality, it is easy to see how many of our actions, lack of actions, and attitudes are tainted by sin.

We see from Scripture not only that all of us have sin in our lives but also that the result of that sin is spiritual separation from God, both now and for eternity. As Romans 6:23 declares, "the wages of sin is death." The Christian understanding, then, is that if we really got what we deserve—if the saying "What goes around comes around" were true—we would be lost.

The good news, however, is that Jesus came to live the perfect life that we could never live, and He died the death that we rightly deserve. Arguably, the most well-known verse in Scripture is John 3:16, "For God so loved the world, that he gave his only Son, that whoever believes in him should not perish but have eternal life." The gap between us and God that we are unable to bridge because of our sin has been filled by Jesus' life, death, and resurrection. Ephesians 2:8-9 explains it this way: "By grace you have been saved through faith. And this is not your own doing; it is the gift of God, not a result of works, so that no one may boast." We didn't earn our salvation; it is a gift from God by His grace, which we receive as we put our faith in Him.

The result of our faith in His gift is that we who were by nature children of wrath (Ephesians 2:3) have now become adopted children of God (Galatians 4:5-7). John 1:12 sums up the gospel of Jesus when the writer says, "But to all who did receive him, who believed in his name, he gave the right to become children of God." Adoption is a powerful image of what has changed in our relationship with God. We were brought into the family of God not based on our credentials, but based on the love and desire of the Father.

This image of adoption is personally powerful for me. I was adopted when I was two days old. My parents didn't adopt me because of what I had done. They also didn't adopt me because of how good of a person I was going to become. No, they made me their son, they gave me their name, they promised to care for and nurture me no matter what simply because they wanted a child. And there is nothing I could ever do to make them love me more or less.

My guess is that since you are reading a book on how to disciple other people, you know the above truths. The questions, however, are whether or not our identity, actions, security, and even motivation for our actions are centered in the above truths. In order to illustrate this question, we need to look at the first quality in the discipleship assessment.

QUALITY #1: Gospel-Saturated Life

The extent to which a person's identity and actions are motivated by who they are in Christ.

The first core quality is that of the gospel-saturated life. This quality is defined as the extent to which the identity, motivation, and actions of the individual are connected to who they are in Christ. Within the larger quality of the gospel-saturated life, there are two subordinated characteristics: *gospel-centered identity* and *gospel-centered actions*.

Characteristic #1: *Gospel-Centered Identity*

The extent to which an individual bases their identity upon who they are in Jesus and what He has done for them.

How does one know whether their core identity is centered in the truth of the gospel or something else? The key is where a person gets their sense of worth. How do they feel when they achieve certain accomplishments? It is appropriate to feel good about our achievements, but do they define us? If a person needs to brag about their victories or constantly give their résumé, that is an indication that these accomplishments are their source of identity.

We get another sense of where our identity lies when we fail at something. No one likes to fail, and no one enjoys failure. But sometimes, people can be so crippled by failure because their identity, their sense of who they are, is so tied to their achievement. When they fail, it can result in anger toward others or self-loathing.

Several decades ago, I knew a man I'll call Peter. Peter was a visiting professor in the sciences at a university in the United States and attended a local church. He had a wife and a two-year-old son. Peter was accomplished in his field and had a generous grant to do some innovative research for several years. He was invited to present his research at a large international symposium. At the conference, his work received some very harsh critique by colleagues. Peter was so distraught by the critique he received that on his way back to the United States, he went into the airplane bathroom and took his life. Peter's identity was so tied to his work that when his work was challenged, his identity was shaken to its core.

There are certainly less extreme and more common examples. I have seen parents, particularly stay-at-home mothers, whose identity and worth were inextricably tied to their children. When their children didn't measure up, not only were they disappointed, but they also felt it was a personal reflection on their own worth and value. I saw a woman—a pillar of the church where her adult child was a member—leave her husband and family for another man. Her parents were not only distraught but also concerned—understandably, as this situation reflected upon them. They met with their pastor, who continued to draw them to their identity as adopted children of God. If their identity was truly rooted in who they were in Jesus, they could still be sad and grieve the situation with their daughter, but it wouldn't affect their self-image. After some time had passed, these parents were able to put the situation with their daughter in proper perspective in light of who they were in Jesus. It was a great source of encouragement to other parents to take their identity from Jesus and not from the success or failure of their children.

Having a successful career or a wonderful family is not a bad thing. In fact, these gifts are God given. The challenge is when these good things become the ultimate things, when these achievements become the basis for our identity. Those who are in professional ministry are just as tempted—if not more so—to take their identity from their work in the church. If the church or ministry isn't doing as well as they would hope, pastors are tempted to feel as if they are disappointing God or to question their sense of self. Conversely, if things are going well, the church is growing, and people are coming to faith, pastors are tempted to take their identity from how well the church is doing.

The reality is, however, that when we become followers of Jesus, not only are we adopted children of God but we are also clothed with the righteousness of Christ. I love the hymn "On Christ the Solid Rock I Stand." I am always moved when I sing the line "Dressed in His righteousness alone, Faultless to stand before the throne." If I am dressed in the righteousness of Christ, it means that when God looks at me, He doesn't just see a man whose sins are washed away. He sees the credentials and righteousness of Christ laid upon me. And if God looks at me and sees the righteousness of Christ, then I must ask myself, What could I possibly add to my résumé on top of the credentials of Jesus? God isn't impressed with how big my church is or how great my kids are. I can't add anything to my résumé because I already have it all in Christ. At the same time, nothing I do could diminish the fact that the credentials of Christ are laid upon me.

If nothing I could do can make God more impressed with me, and nothing I could do can diminish that the righteous credentials of Christ are laid upon me, then this should be the basis for my identity. It is challenging to remember this when there are so many factors at work that hinder us from living out of our identity as beloved children of God. We contend with the pressures and desires of other people; we are in a culture that wants to assign our value based upon our accomplishments.

In order to combat this mentality, we must continually saturate ourselves in the gospel of Jesus. Sometimes, we think it is just unbelievers that need to hear the gospel. The reality is that we all need to be reminded of who we are in Jesus as saved, redeemed, reconciled, and adopted sons and daughters of the King.

Characteristic #2: *Gospel-Centered Actions*

The extent to which a disciple's actions are motivated by who they are in Christ.

There are two ways in which our actions can fail to be gospel centered. These two ways go back to the story of the Prodigal Son. The younger brother took his position with the father for granted and used the riches of the father to live an immoral life. Unfortunately, there are times when those who profess to be Christians take for granted the grace of God and use forgiveness as a license to continue to disobey the desires of God. The apostle Paul addresses this when he postulates in Romans 6:1: "What shall we say then? Are we to continue in sin that grace may abound?" His answer is "By no means!" (verse 2)—or, as I translate, "Heck no!"

If we are saturated in the gospel, we are more obedient to the will and desire of God. For example, if we are saturated in the gospel, we will be so overwhelmed by the generosity of God that we will be more generous with our own finances and time toward God's work in the world. If we are overwhelmed by the faithfulness of God toward us, we will naturally have increasing fidelity in our marriages and in other commitments that we have made. If we are caught up with the forgiveness of God toward us, it will lead us toward taking a forgiving posture toward others.

One way to have actions that are not gospel centered is to be disobedient to the will of God. The other way we can fall short of living gospel-centered lives is to do the right actions but for the wrong reasons. This is the older-brother syndrome, and it is more difficult to see in our lives and in the lives of others. It is just as important to uncover, though, as it is a major hindrance to discipleship. Jesus' woes to the Pharisees at the end of Matthew 23 are a great example. In verses 27 and 28, He says,

> *Woe to you, scribes and Pharisees, hypocrites! For you are like whitewashed tombs, which outwardly appear beautiful, but within are full of dead people's bones and all uncleanness. So you also outwardly appear righteous to others, but within you are full of hypocrisy and lawlessness.*

Jesus' critique is obvious: The Pharisees look great on the outside, they are engaging in the right religious practices, and yet their hearts are dead and their souls are empty. Sometimes we can go through the right motions and have great outward appearances and our religiosity can be very impressive to others, but our empty works can be as filthy rags (Isaiah 64:6, NIV).

We can do the right things for the wrong reasons as we try to prove the depth of our faith before others. Jesus gives great warnings about practicing our righteousness before others with the hope of drawing attention to ourselves. In Matthew 6, He warns against making a spectacle about our giving to seek acclamation. He warns against praying in such a way that draws attention to what wonderful prayers we are.

Sometimes we can even do the right things in order to prove our worth to God; our good work—rather than the grace of Jesus—then becomes the foundation of identity. In Luke 18, Jesus tells a parable "to some who trusted in themselves that they were righteous, and treated others with contempt" (verse 9). So the purpose of this parable is to chasten those who were basing their identity in their good works and not in the grace of God. He goes on to tell the story in verses 10-14:

> Two men went up into the temple to pray, one a Pharisee and the other a tax collector. The Pharisee, standing by himself, prayed thus: "God, I thank you that I am not like other men, extortioners, unjust, adulterers, or even like this tax collector. I fast twice a week; I give tithes of all that I get." But the tax collector, standing far off, would not even lift up his eyes to heaven, but beat his breast, saying, "God, be merciful to me, a sinner!" I tell you, this man went down to his house justified, rather than the other. For everyone who exalts himself will be humbled, but the one who humbles himself will be exalted.

The tax collector was justified; he was made right by God because he admitted his sin and trusted in God's grace. The Pharisee not only had a disdain for the tax collector but also trusted in his works rather than God's grace, so he was not justified. Sometimes we are tempted to look at how hard we have volunteered for the church, how much money we have given, or any number of other things, and we are tempted to use those things as the basis for our own self-justification. Deep down, we think we might not actually need a savior because we consider our good works good enough.

What often happens is that other core areas of discipleship are interrelated to this quality of a gospel-saturated life. For example, the first time I took the assessment, I scored lower in areas related to patience. As I dug deeper, I realized that there were ways in which I was trying to prove my worth to God and others, and I was impatient because I wanted to prove my identity. While the presenting issue was my lack of patience, the deeper issue was failing to take my identity in who I am in Christ. As you look at the strengths and growth opportunities in your own discipleship, consider potential links to this particular quality of a gospel-saturated life.

Gospel-centered actions is one of the most challenging qualities to identify in our own lives and in the lives of others. Like Chuck, there are many individuals who are expressing the type of behavior we encourage in the church. The behaviors can be motivated not by the grace of Jesus Christ but rather to earn the approval of God, others, or even ourselves. However, when we truly discover the depth by which we have been loved and received, it will not only change the actions of some people but will also change the attitudes behind those actions.

REFLECTION QUESTIONS

1. What image of salvation in Scripture is most meaningful for you? (For example, being adopted, forgiven, redeemed, saved, or reconciled.)

2. How does this image of salvation influence your approach to life?

3. What are clues that reveal whether your actions are gospel motivated or selfishly motivated?

4. Where are places other than Jesus that you might tend to base your identity on?

5. How can the gospel help you when you realize that you are placing your worth in something other than Jesus?

CHAPTER 4

Qualities of the Heart

The Character of a Disciple

WHEN THE ELDERS AT the local community church were look-ing for a new pastor, they created lists of the qualities that they hoped the new pastor would possess. High on this list of qualities was "being a good biblical teacher." They were in an educated community with a fair amount of faculty and staff from the nearby prestigious university. Comments from the elders and congregation included "We want our pastor to have a PhD," "We'd like the pastor to preach through books of the Bible," and "We want to hear the meanings of words from Greek and Hebrew."

The community church saw the task of making disciples as synonymous with educating the members of the church. The thought was that the more the people know about the Bible, the better disciples they make.

One member did offer a different opinion. She said, "I read somewhere once that many churches are educated beyond their obedience. I think that quote might apply to our church." She went on to explain that if the church held seminars on the Bible or other religions, they would get a lot of positive response. But, the member pointed out, the few times the church did twenty-four-hour prayer vigils, the church would only see 2 to 3 percent of their people attend over the course of the event. Further, she noted, people never came to learn about prayer or other spiritual disciplines. She ended by saying, "I know that we know a lot about the Bible. Obviously, knowing the Bible is important. I just, I just wonder . . . how well we are living it." The room was silent, but all were pondering the validity of her comments.

In Western culture, especially since the age of enlightenment, we have often associated being a mature disciple with knowing the Bible. Knowing the Bible is important—in fact, that is one of the core qualities on our profile of a disciple. It is not the only characteristic, however, and the mere knowledge of Scripture does not a disciple make. If we excel in the area of biblical knowledge and fail to have the character and depth of relationship with Jesus, we can become dangerous.

We see Paul's warning against overvaluing human knowledge in 1 Corinthians 8:1: "Now concerning food offered to idols: we know that 'all of us possess knowledge.' This 'knowledge' puffs up, but love builds up." Knowledge can make us prideful, which is, of course, inconsistent with God's desire for our lives. When I graduated from seminary, the speaker for our class in the School of Theology was Ken Fong. I clearly remember him saying that he never hires new seminary graduates. He will hire people before they go to seminary and a few years after seminary, but never right out of seminary. This was a very discouraging speech for people who were about to walk across the stage and graduate! But his rationale was good. "Brand-new seminary graduates can have what I call PGA, Postgraduation Arrogance." He said that before seminary, people don't think they know it all, and three or four years after seminary, they *know* that they don't know it all. But right after seminary, the new seminary graduate might think that they know everything. He said sometimes, it is even as if the new seminary graduate feels like they bring God with them to their first position.

While Ken was talking to recent seminary graduates, we know that pride, arrogance, and the like can impact any Christian, full-time ministry worker or not. We all need to make sure that we are loving the Lord with all of our hearts, that our hearts are made right with God.

It has been stated previously that the first three qualities of a disciple are associated with the heart. We have already explored the first one: a gospel-saturated life. The second quality has to do with nurturing our relationship with God through prayer, being changed by His Word, and incorporating other spiritual practices so that our relationship with God can flourish. The third quality relates to our character and is a distillation of the fruit of the Spirit. In the rest of this chapter, we will expand on qualities 2 and 3.

QUALITY #2: Connected to God

The extent to which this individual is in a growing relationship with God through His Word, prayer, and other disciplines.

I give two copies of Gary Chapman's book *The 5 Love Languages* to every couple that I counsel premaritally.[1] I encourage the couple to read the book and then take some time to identify how each other gives and receives love. One of those love languages is *quality time*. While some people have quality time as the primary way they like to be shown love, this quality is vitally important to any marriage. Those date nights, lunch dates, and weekends away are so refreshing and life giving for a healthy marriage. They help us stay connected to our spouses. The way we spend that quality time might look different. Quality time can be moments of intensive conversations or desperation during the valleys of life. Sometimes, there are moments of laughter and frivolity. Whatever the case, a healthy marriage needs a well-balanced diet of quality time.

Quality time is also an important characteristic in our relationship with God. Just as I need quality time to keep my marriage strong, so I need quality time with God to become more intimate with Him. In order to have that quality time, I must have regular times of connection and closeness to the Lord. This well-balanced, well-rounded diet of practices is vitally important to maintaining and growing our connection to God. There are some standard practices that we must continually engage, such as regular times of prayer and reflecting on Scripture. There are other exercises we can do—classically called the *spiritual disciplines* or *spiritual practices*—that can enhance our life with the Lord.

Characteristic #1: *Prayer*

The extent to which an individual engages in a deep prayer life that involves both talking and listening to the Lord.

The health of a disciple's prayer life is measured by a few key behaviors. A disciple with a healthy prayer life will first and foremost spend regular time with the Lord in prayer where the person not only communicates to God but also listens to His leading and direction. We all know that we are to speak to God in prayer, but we probably spend much less time listening to God.

There are several passages of Scripture that outline the importance of taking a listening posture toward God. Psalm 85 is a great psalm that is written to ask the Lord to revive His people. Verse 8 says, "Let me hear what God the LORD will speak, for he will speak peace to his people, to his saints." The writer expresses a desire to ask the Lord to speak and a commitment to hear what He has to say. We see an example of this kind of commitment in Luke 10:39 with Mary, who was not consumed with business but instead listened at the feet of the Lord. We can often be so consumed by laying things at God's feet that we forget to be receptive to His response. We might not give the Lord the opportunity to open our eyes to new things, directions, and insights.

In looking at prayer life, we also want to examine how quickly we are willing to go to God in prayer as opposed to trying to solve the situation on our own. I was walking with a colleague a few years ago, and we passed by a homeless man with some significant mental-health issues. He appeared to have been a veteran and was acting as if he thought he was still at war: He was yelling at people and speaking into his nonexistent radio asking for reinforcements. When we were walking by this man, I certainly felt bad for him, but I was also worried about the safety of myself and my female colleague. I noticed that as I walked by, my hands naturally clenched into fists, as though I might have to protect us. My colleague's hands, however, were folded in prayer while she prayed for him and for us.

Those were two very different gut reactions to the situation, and they were indicative of how we both tend to solve situations. I tend to jump into "fix it" mode and try to figure out a solution on my own. She tends to go to God when faced with challenges and opportunities. Healthy disciples will go to the Lord quickly—both in times of trial and in times of peace—to see how the Lord is leading. Healthy disciples heed the Word of God from Proverbs 3:5-6:

> Trust in the LORD with all your heart,
>> and do not lean on your own understanding.
> In all your ways acknowledge him,
>> and he will make straight your paths.

Characteristic #2: *Connecting with God through His Word*

*The extent to which the individual engages the
Lord through Scripture.*

When we engage Scripture, we do so from two different yet synergistic perspectives. On the one hand, we want to learn more about God, ourselves, and His work in the world. But we also want to engage with God's Word as a way to connect with Him. The former approach to learning about God will be talked about in the next chapter. In this chapter, we will focus on engaging with God's Word as an avenue to listen to and grow closer to the Lord.

Measuring healthy engagement with God through His Word involves several different aspects. First, we want to know if the person is spending time connecting with God through His Word. It is easy—especially for pastors and those who have been Christians for a long time—to stop reading the Scriptures as a devotional exercise and only read His Word when preparing lessons and Bible studies. They can sometimes have the false thought (though it probably wouldn't be said out loud) that they are beyond needing to read the Bible, that they know the stories and what the Scriptures say. It is still important to read the Scriptures devotionally, as the Lord may want to reveal new insights or we might find ourselves connecting with a different portion of the text. For example, there are times when I have read the story of the Prodigal Son (Luke 15) and found myself identifying with the son who has left; other times, I have seen myself as the older brother in the story. Reading Scripture to determine what God wants to say to me at this point in my life is a crucial posture before the Lord.

Sometimes, we claim we are "too busy" to engage in devotional reading of God's Word. People can be under the impression that they will not get as much out of reading God's Word on their own as they would hearing their pastor explain the passage. Like baby birds that require their mother to digest the worm and regurgitate it to her children, these individuals require the preacher to digest God's Word and regurgitate it for them. They then become stunted in their Christian growth and their ability to hear from God directly.

I often find that in orthodox and evangelical streams of Christianity, we have a very high view of the nature and authority of Scripture to teach truth. What we can often lack is true hunger for God to feed us and quench our souls' thirst through His Word.

I know it is a challenge in my life. I love food. I love the taste; I love the satisfaction. In my younger years, I used to see the world as "all you can eat," and I would accept the challenge of getting my money's worth. I was challenged by Jesus' words when tempted by the enemy: "Man shall not live by bread alone, but by every word that comes from the mouth of God" (Matthew 4:4). I would have to ask myself, Do I crave the Word of God like I crave food? Can I experience the satisfaction that I get through food by engaging with what has come out of the mouth of God? This is my prayer for myself, that I would continually crave the Word of God and be satisfied by it at least as much as, and preferably more than, I am by food.

Characteristic #3: *Incorporating Other Disciplines*

The extent to which the individual utilizes a variety of spiritual disciplines in their relationship with the Lord.

The habit of incorporating other spiritual disciplines into one's life seems foreign to a lot of Christians. A simple definition of *spiritual disciplines* is incorporating various practices into your life that can aid in your growth as a disciple. For example,

I mentioned that I love to eat, and I frequently find that I crave food more than I crave the Word of God. This is a great time for me to incorporate a discipline of fasting. I don't fast to please God, earn His approval, or impress Him with how spiritual I am; I fast to reset my spiritual life and retrain my soul to find that satisfaction in God rather than in food.

The spiritual disciplines can also be added in your life when you find that your spiritual life has become stale or routine. Those are great times to incorporate a new practice for a while to bring freshness to your connection with God.

There are many available books that walk through a variety of spiritual disciplines. One of my favorites is *Spiritual Disciplines Handbook* by Adele Ahlberg Calhoun.[2] This book is invaluable because not only does it give you a fairly extensive list of spiritual practices but it also helps you determine which spiritual practices might be helpful given your particular situation. As an example, there are times where we can sense that we are seeking to find our happiness through purchasing things. In this case, the discipline of simplicity might be very helpful. Other times, we might feel as if we are busy and running around like the proverbial chicken with its head cut off. In these instances, we might want to try the disciplines of Sabbath or slowness.

It is not the intention for this characteristic to become legalistic. It could be tempting, for example, to want to score higher on this aspect of the discipleship assessment and try to cram in as many spiritual disciplines as possible. What this characteristic really seeks to measure, however, is whether or not we are intentional about our approach to our own spiritual health and vitality. Are we seeking new ways to grow and develop as disciples? Are we developing a plan for our own spiritual growth and development? When we approach other spiritual disciplines as a blessing to enhance our own discipleship, we will be much healthier and satisfied, and our spiritual vitality will not feel like a burden.

QUALITY #3: Exhibiting the Fruit of the Spirit

The extent to which an individual expresses a life marked by the fruit of the Spirit.

The last quality having to do with matters of the heart is related to our character. The characteristics for this quality are taken from the fruit of the Spirit, which is described in Galatians chapter 5. Paul says, "The fruit of the Spirit is love, joy, peace, patience, kindness, goodness, faithfulness, gentleness, self-control; against such things there is no law" (verses 22-23). This passage has some parallels with the great commandment in Matthew 22:37-41. In the great commandment, Jesus says that on the two commandments of loving God and loving others hang the Law and the Prophets. Again, His point was that if you live out these two commandments, you will be living out the other commandments by default. In Galatians 5, Paul says something similar: If you allow the Spirit of God to produce this fruit, there will be no law. This is to say that if you exhibit this fruit, you will be living in accordance with the law.

As we went through the process of validating the simple discipleship assessment, we began with evaluating each one of these characteristics separately. We found that these nine aspects could be grouped into four larger categories.

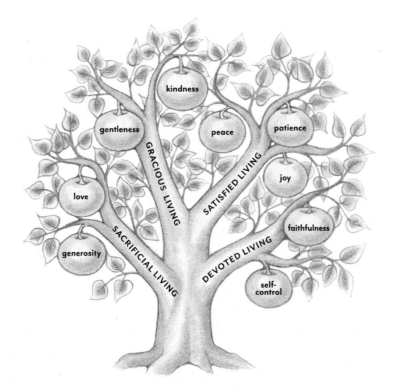

Characteristic #1: *Sacrificial Living*

The extent to which the individual exhibits the sacrificial nature of Jesus toward others.

Sacrificial living incorporates the fruits of love and generosity. The word *love* that is used in the fruit of the Sprit passage is *agape*. This is distinct from other types of love, such as *philos*, which is a brotherly love, and *eros*, which is the love held between a husband and wife. Agape is the type of love that is used to describe the self-sacrificing nature of Jesus, particularly as He gave His life for us on the cross.

Generosity also has at its core an element of sacrifice. It is true that someone who is a multimillionaire could be very generous with her money and not feel a pinch; however, for most people who are going to be generous with their time and money, this experience will involve an element of sacrifice.

Sacrificial living involves giving up valuable resources. If we are truly sacrificial, we will do these things even for those who will not be able to repay us in the future or help us advance a personal agenda. I find it most difficult to be sacrificial for those who have been unkind or flat-out mean to me. The call of Jesus is to love our enemies (Matthew 5:43-48). He continues, asking, What virtue is it if you love someone and give to someone who can repay or return the favor?

There is a link between all of these fruits of the Spirit and the gospel-centered actions described in the previous chapter. Sacrificial living doesn't come from simply trying harder, but from being overwhelmed by the sacrificial nature of Jesus. He gave up everything to live the life we could never live and die the death we rightly deserved. And, as Paul says in Romans 5:8, Jesus did all of this while we were sinners. He did this while we were enemies of God and rightly deserved His wrath. In 1 John 4:7-12, John tells us that our motivation and ability to love others comes from God's sacrificial love for us. He says, "Let us love one another, for love is from God" (verse 7), and further, that "anyone who does not love does not know God, because God is love" (verse 8). The more deeply we know the love of God, the more deeply we will be able to love one another, and the more our sacrificial living seems like no sacrifice at all.

Characteristic #2: *Gracious Living*

The extent to which an individual exhibits care, humility, and compassion when interacting with others.

Gracious living is comprised of the fruits of kindness and gentleness. The word "kindness," *chrestotes* in Greek,[3] is primarily used in the New Testament to describe a virtuous human attribute. There is, however, one time that the word is used to describe an attribute of God: In Romans 2:4, Paul says, "Do you presume on the riches of his kindness and forbearance and patience, not knowing that God's kindness is meant to lead you to repentance?" In this situation, the kindness of God is His ability to not bestow on us the punishment that we rightfully deserve. Instead, He is kind enough to delay giving us what we rightly deserve, so as to offer us an opportunity to repent. The kindness of God, therefore, is a manifestation of His grace, thereby falling into the category of gracious living.

Gentleness is indeed similar to kindness, in that it is primarily used to denote a human attribute rather than to describe God. One time where the word is used to describe Jesus is when He comes into Jerusalem on a donkey. Matthew quotes Zechariah 9:9: "Say to the daughter of Zion, 'Behold, your king is coming to you, humble, and mounted on a donkey, on a colt, the foal of a beast of burden'" (Matthew 21:5). The word *humble* in that passage is the same Greek word that is translated as "gentle." The point is that when Jesus came into Jerusalem, He didn't come for war, but for peace. He came in a spirit of humility rather than pride. This act of gentleness and humility is an aspect of gracious living. It was Jesus' willingness to put aside His rights and privileges to show His gracious posture.

When we are gracious, we are willing to not act out of anger, even when we have every earthly right to be angry. When we are gracious, we are willing to forgive and let go of the wrongs that have been done to us and display mercy and forgiveness to others, and we embody a desire to use our speech to build up—rather than rip apart—others in the body of Christ. When we are living graciously, we want to make others feel valued and important rather than seeking to gain the upper hand with them.

Characteristic #3: *Satisfied Living*

The extent to which the individual is able to live a joyful, nonanxious life in the midst of all circumstances.

Satisfied living measures our ability to be content and at peace rather than always thinking the grass is greener on the other side of the fence. Three fruits are included in this characteristic: peace, joy, and patience, all of which are related to our internal temperament. We think again of Paul as a great example of this: Even in the midst of extreme hardship, he maintains a positive attitude. He is able to do this not because he is naive or oblivious to the challenges around him, but because he can look at his own circumstances in light of the greater truth the Lord provides. This allows Paul to say things like "I consider that the sufferings of this present time are not worth comparing with the glory that is to be revealed to us" (Romans 8:18). Paul is fully aware that the challenges around him are many, and he has had to suffer greatly because of the gospel. However, he knows that if he looks at his situation compared to the glory of the Lord, it will give him a whole different perspective, one that allows him to be at peace and exude joy.

This characteristic is honestly one of the hardest in my own discipleship. I like to get things done; I like to be busy; I like to be efficient. I have a friend who coaches executives on the StrengthsFinder tool.[4] When he meets people who have taken the StrengthsFinder, he asks them to disclose their top five strengths. Then, as if he were psychic, he begins to tell them about their personalities in amazing detail. When I first met him and shared my strengths, he said, among other things, "Let me guess. You like to set high goals for yourself. If you don't meet those goals, you beat yourself up. If you meet your goals, you get upset with yourself for not setting high enough goals." Oh my goodness—he nailed me!

While setting goals can be a very positive thing, our joy and satisfaction should not be measured by whether we meet our goals. And we certainly shouldn't be in a no-win situation where we are deprived of joy or peace because we are either unhappy that we missed our goals or unhappy that we didn't make big enough goals.

The comforting thing is that while living a satisfied life is not easy, it is something that can be learned. In Philippians 4:12, Paul says, "I know how to be brought low, and I know how to abound. In any and every circumstance, I have learned the secret of facing plenty and hunger, abundance and need." It is a learning experience to see God's greater truth in the midst of our earthly circumstances.

Characteristic #4: *Devoted Living*

The extent to which an individual remains faithful to their commitments to God, others, and themselves.

Devoted living is all about keeping the general and specific commitments we have made, especially in the midst of different temptations. The fruits associated with this characteristic are faithfulness and self-control. Faithfulness is at the very core of who God is. God keeps His Word and His promises to us. If God were not faithful, then we wouldn't be able to trust His Word, because God might change His mind or break His promises. In 1 John 1:9, John says, "If we confess our sins, he is faithful and just to forgive us our sins and to cleanse us from all unrighteousness." John is illustrating that one of the attributes of God is His faithfulness to do what He says He is going to do; hence, John says that because God is faithful, He will forgive our sins if we confess them before Him. God has promised this throughout Scripture, and because He is a faithful God, we can trust His promises.

We also know that Jesus was able to exhibit self-control and stay devoted to God's call in His life. Hebrews 4:15 says, "We do not have a high priest who is unable to sympathize with our weaknesses, but one who in every respect has been tempted as we are, yet without sin." In the garden of Gethsemane, we see Jesus ask the Father if there was another way for His will to be accomplished, and yet He submitted to the plan of the Father and went to the cross.

We all make general and specific commitments. We make

commitments to the Lord when we receive Jesus as our Lord and Savior and follow Him no matter where He leads. We make commitments to follow His Word even when—especially when—we desire the opposite. We make commitments to our spouses, parents, coworkers, and friends. We have opportunities to break those commitments, perhaps even when no one is watching. The question with this characteristic is whether we will keep our commitments, and if we do occasionally let people down, whether we are willing to accept responsibility and own up to our faults.

What excites me about the qualities of the heart as they relate to the simple discipleship assessment is that they offer a way to quantify our spiritual health in these areas. It is exciting to have others express the ways they see us connect to the Lord and the ways in which the fruit of the Spirit is manifested in our lives. I encourage you to answer the questions provided to reflect on these qualities of the heart before going to the next chapter.

REFLECTION QUESTIONS

1. At what time in your life did you feel the most connected to God?

2. How do you typically connect with God?

3. Have you ever tried a spiritual discipline (such as fasting)? If so, how was that experience?

4. As you look at the four categories within the fruit of the Spirit, which one tends to include areas of strength? Which might present a growth opportunity?

5. How do you understand the link between the first characteristic of the gospel-saturated life and the fruit of the Spirit?

CHAPTER 5

Qualities of the Mind

The Knowledge of a Disciple

A BIBLE-STUDY GROUP AT Christ Community Church was studying the end of John 8. As the group read verse 58, where Jesus says, "Truly, truly, I say to you, before Abraham was, I am," a robust dialogue broke out about the nature of Jesus. One person said, "I thought Jesus was God's Son, not God." Someone else said, "I think Jesus was God and then stopped being God when He came to earth." Another member said, "I think Jesus was half God and half human." Further conversations revolved around why Jesus died and whether He had to die or if that was simply an unfortunate ending to His ministry.

These conversations spun into larger conversations about the nature of God. One member said, "Well, if Jesus is God, then I like Jesus better than the God of the Old Testament.

I can relate to Jesus. He is so much nicer than God, who orders the killing of innocent children." Another member responded, "I don't think God actually ordered that; I think people thought it was God, so they wrote that in the Bible, but I can't imagine it really happened that way."

After Bible study was over, informal conversations continued while the group was enjoying their coffee and dessert. Several remarked that it was a good discussion and it was great that there were so many opinions expressed; however, Sue, the leader of the group, was discouraged by the lack of understanding and called the pastor the next morning to discuss the situation.

The previous chapter warned against being so focused on the mind and biblical knowledge that we miss a relationship with Jesus. The opposite can also be true. We can be so focused on a generic spirituality yet fail to have our faith firmly linked to the truth. This chapter will therefore focus on the core quality related to our minds.

In my role as a denominational leader, I get to interact with leaders of other denominations. These are fabulous brothers and sisters in Christ who love the Lord and His work in the Kingdom. There are times when we have robust conversations around theological differences, but we always know that we hold to the same core truth of the Christian faith. Neither this book nor the companion assessment assumes one stream of Christian theology. We are committed to ensuring that disciples share the central teachings of the Christian faith. Disagreement about core issues of doctrine such as the person and work of Jesus, the triune nature of God, and the authority of Scripture are not merely matters of theological opinion. Disciples not only know and adhere to the essentials of the Christian faith but also are able to articulate them to others.

God continually lifts the value of His Word and calls us to understand it more deeply. Recall Hebrews 5 (mentioned in chapter 1), where the author asserts that the whole community should be qualified to teach other believers. They do not have this ability, however, because they "no longer try to understand" (verse 11, NIV). We know the importance of authority and its ability to produce life in us. As 2 Timothy 3:16-17 says, "All Scripture is breathed out by God and profitable for teaching, for reproof, for correction, and for training in righteousness, that the man of God may be complete, equipped for every good work." Hebrews 4:12 puts it this way: "The word of God is living and active, sharper than any two-edged sword, piercing to the division of soul and of spirit, of joints and of marrow, and discerning the thoughts and intentions of the heart."

Given these Scripture passages, along with many others, we have several responsibilities. We are to know God's Word because it is the authority in our lives. We are to allow God's Word to change and mold us. We are to assimilate scriptural teaching on important subjects to inform our comprehensive theology. We are to be able to teach God's Word to others. This fourth quality helps us understand how we are to love God with our minds.

QUALITY #4: Understanding the Bible and Christian Theology

The extent to which the individual studies and understands the significant themes of the Bible and applies them to his or her own life.

There are four supporting characteristics associated with this quality. The first two are having a working knowledge of the Old and New Testaments, respectively. Disciples don't need to be biblical scholars; however, having a general depth of knowledge about the Scriptures is important and should be expected of a disciple. The third characteristic has to do with having theological knowledge about the core doctrines of the Christian faith. The final characteristic is related to a disciple's ability to study God's Word. Is the disciple able to dig into the Scriptures and use basic resources to distill truth and apply it to their life?

Characteristic #1: *Old Testament Literacy*

The extent to which an individual understands and comprehends the major themes of the Old Testament and how it fits into the totality of God's story.

When Paul wrote to Timothy about the nature of Scripture, the only Scriptures that he was talking about were the Hebrew Scriptures of the Old Testament. It is certainly appropriate to apply Paul's words to the New Testament, as well, but his particular focus in this passage was on the nature of the Old Testament. Throughout centuries, debates have gone on about the status of the Old Testament. Some have wanted the

Old Testament removed from the biblical canon; others have wanted to interpret it through the lens of the New Testament. The church, however, has consistently seen the Old Testament as part of God's Holy Scriptures, and it is no less important, valuable, or true than the New Testament.

It is important to view the Old Testament as the foundation for the New Testament. Jesus and the New Testament writers frequently quote the Old Testament to show its fulfillment in the life and work of Jesus or to reinforce a theological point. For example, in Luke 4, we see when Jesus reads from the prophet Isaiah about the nature of the coming Messiah. Here Jesus is using the Old Testament to announce and assert the reality of who He is. In Romans 3, Paul pulls many Old Testament passages together to demonstrate the reality that no one is blameless before God—all need a Savior.

The Old Testament provides great lessons and wisdom for us. The Psalms show people interacting with God in a very real and deep way in a variety of situations. No matter what someone is going through in life, they would be hard-pressed not to be able to find a psalm that speaks to their particular situation. There are also wonderful moral lessons and examples in the Old Testament. For example, the multiple stories of David not only show his good qualities but also prove that even a king needs a Savior. In Genesis, stories of the patriarchs give further examples of God's faithfulness through the generations. Even more challenging books like Leviticus can help us see how God desires holiness in our lives. Even though many of the ritual laws of the Old Testament have been fulfilled in Christ, they still reveal God's desire for us to look to Him amid even the most mundane activities.

The Old Testament also not only sets up our need for Christ and salvation by grace but also gives us glimpses of God's grace even before Christ was revealed. The first story of humans making sacrifices to God is that of Cain and Abel in Genesis 4. In this instance, Cain offers the Lord what he produces and his sacrifice is rejected. Meanwhile, Abel offers the Lord an animal sacrifice. With this sacrifice, Abel is admitting that there is nothing he can do to earn his place with God. This is why God accepts Abel's sacrifice and not Cain's. It is an illustration from the very beginning that the restoration of our relationship with God must result from His gift to us, not our works. Throughout the Old Testament, we continue to see sacrifices made to God. This practice may seem barbaric to a modern reader, but these sacrifices help us understand the need for the final sacrifice of Jesus.

It is important, therefore, to continue to study the Old Testament, both for itself—to hear what God is saying to us directly—and with the grand narrative of God's story and redemptive purposes in mind . . . which leads to our study of the New Testament.

Characteristic #2: *New Testament Literacy*

The extent to which an individual understands and comprehends the New Testament and allows it to shape and mold their life.

It is likely not a difficult task to defend the notion that disciples of Jesus need to have knowledge of the New Testament. Yet even in our very educated society, many Christians have a limited understanding of the New Testament. Sometimes this limited understanding leads people to take verses out of context or make conclusions about the nature of Jesus based on one or two proof texts. I can't tell you how many times I hear things like "We aren't supposed to judge people" in conversations about what it means to have transformed behavior. Speakers quote the New Testament, saying, "[Jesus said,] Judge not, that you be not judged" (Matthew 7:1).

What people fail to realize is that there is a difference between *judgment* and *discernment*. Jesus is telling us that it is not our job to pronounce ultimate sentence on a person; that is God's job alone. But we certainly need to discern right from wrong and help others do the same. In fact, a few verses later in Matthew, Jesus tells us to not cast our pearls before swine. In other words, some judging is needed to determine where to spend our energy for the gospel. In the great commission at the end of Matthew 28, Jesus tells us to "make disciples of all nations" by "teaching them to observe all that [he has] commanded" (verses 19-20). If we are going to teach people to obey, then certainly we will need to tell them the difference between right and wrong. A misunderstanding about Jesus' teaching on judgment is just one example, but it illustrates the challenges we face when we have a limited understanding of the New Testament.

An understanding of the New Testament involves knowing the books it contains, as well as its basic background information and general purpose. As we were developing the simple discipleship assessment, we had several discussions about how much a person should know as a disciple. In the end, we concluded that disciples should know the books in the New

Testament and have a good working knowledge of their contents to lay a very important foundation for faith.

New Testament understanding also incorporates discerning the nature and character of Jesus. Can a person recognize Jesus' character and how He calls them to respond in various situations? Depending on your age, you might remember the popular wristbands and T-shirts that said "WWJD," which stood for "What Would Jesus Do?" This trend became popular and then was criticized for being trendy. The question, however, is a great one. How much better a world would we live in if everyone asked this question before acting? How much better might our churches be if we all asked this question before acting or speaking?

Characteristic #3: *Growth in Comprehension of Theological Knowledge*

The extent to which the individual comprehends the major Christian doctrines and how their implications impact life.

Christians have traditionally and continually defined themselves by a few core aspects of theology. The first is the nature of the Trinity—an understanding that there is one God who subsists in three persons: Father, Son, and Holy Spirit. Each member of the Trinity is fully divine; no member is less "God" than the others. All three carry the attributes that define the nature of God, and each attribute is equally present among the persons of the Trinity. While a layperson doesn't need to be a theological scholar on the Trinity, it is important that disciples can articulate the Trinity at a basic level. A disciple should be able to articulate the nature of the Trinity and its importance in the life and ministry of the congregation.

The second core aspect of Christian theology is the person and work of Jesus. This foundational truth is inextricably tied to the theology of the Trinity, in that part of understanding the nature of Jesus is understanding that He is fully human and fully divine. This aspect of Jesus is not just interesting but also crucial to understanding the nature of Jesus' death on the cross for us. Only a human could pay the penalty for our sin. Only God could fulfill the righteous requirements of the law to be an appropriate sacrifice for our sin.

The last aspect that Christians often see as foundational to the Christian faith is the authority of the Scriptures. Our understanding of the authority of Scripture is filled with nuances, such as which aspects are literal and which aspects are symbolic but point to a greater-than-literal meaning. For example, some people view the creation narrative as a literal six-day story, while others view it as symbolic epochs of time. Some view it as a story to indicate how the world was created, while others view it as a story about the God behind creation. The basic priority for discipleship is not a disciple's opinion of these topics but whether that disciple views the Bible as authoritative. Do people change their opinions and theology based on the Word of God, or do they change the Word of God to make it fit their desires?

While we don't want to assume the reader is within a particular stream of Christian theology, it is important that a person can grow and wrestle with the finer points of theology, whatever part of the Christian family they belong to. Take, for example, the sovereignty of God. Some traditions carry a very high view regarding the sovereignty of God and His active control in the world; others put more emphasis on human freedom. These two views would lead to different approaches when dealing with people who are facing loss or tragedy. The important aspect here is whether someone wrestles with their theology on these issues and is able to apply it to various situations.

Characteristic #4: *Studying the Word*

The extent to which the individual is able to study and apply the Word of God to their life.

Disciples know how to dig into the Word of God for themselves. One of my pet peeves is when people who have been Christians and going to church for thirty years complain that they aren't "getting fed" at their church. While I certainly believe that the Word of God needs to be preached well during worship, this type of comment implies that the speaker gets their understanding of the Word from other people rather than from digging into it themselves. If we use the analogy that the pastor is a shepherd and those in the congregation are the pastor's flock, then the expectation behind "getting fed" at church breaks down. Unless the sheep are sick or disabled, shepherds don't hand-feed them. The shepherd leads the flock to the food and ensures that they can feed themselves.

The church where I served as an intern had a phenomenal Bible teacher. I was in a small group where we had to answer the ice-breaker question "If you were stranded on an island, what three things would you bring?" One lady said, "My Bible," then paused and said, "Actually, I would bring a cassette player and a case of the pastor's sermons, because I can't understand it on my own."

Healthy disciples are those that can dig into the Word of God themselves. They know the grand story of Scripture and how to find out answers or form opinions based on questions that might arise as they study the Word of God. We live in a time of a phenomenal amount of information, which needs to be read discerningly, but great resources are available to help disciples in their journeys.

As you think through this mind-related quality, take into account that development is a lifelong process and give yourself grace. If you are a new believer, it can be overwhelming to think about building your base of knowledge and your ability to grow in that knowledge. Also give yourself grace if you have been in the church for decades and haven't been attentive to this aspect of your discipleship. The place you are starting from isn't as important as your commitment to grow one step at a time.

REFLECTION QUESTIONS

1. As you read this chapter about the quality of the mind, what stood out to you?

2. Where do you feel particularly confident about your knowledge of the Scriptures?

3. Where do you feel particularly confident about your understanding of basic Christian theology?

4. In what area might you want to gain greater knowledge or confidence? How might you gain that knowledge?

5. How might you respond to a new believer who is overwhelmed by what they don't yet know? Where do you think new believers should start?

CHAPTER 6

Qualities of the Hand, Part 1

The Mission of a Disciple

THE MISSION COMMITTEE OF Main Street Church was setting their budget for the next year. Historically, the church had committed 10 percent of their annual budget to missions. Usually, a third of that money went to mission partners overseas and the remaining two-thirds went to local missions. The church supported about ten local parachurch ministries, such as the local chapter of Habitat for Humanity and a ministry that often helped people with food or other short-term needs. In October, the committee was told that the overall budget for the following year was $600,000. This meant the committee would allocate $60,000 to missions, $40,000 of which would help fund local missions. The committee would ordinarily make these decisions, and then the rest of the year they would hear reports from these organizations and coordinate a periodic service project for the congregation to serve these organizations.

Michelle was a new member of the committee, having just been elected in September. She sheepishly raised her hand in the process and said, "I know I am new on the committee, but I wonder if our committee should be doing more than allocating money to other people who are doing missions." She went on to say, "What if in addition to giving money, our committee helped every person become a missionary in their own neighborhood? What if instead of just doing quarterly service projects, we helped people to see their whole lives as service? What if we helped people actually replicate the ministry of Jesus in their own context?"

Michelle's suggestion sparked an important conversation. What was the role of the church in missions? Was it simply to support other people's mission work? Or was it also to help the congregation see the mission that God had placed upon each one of their lives? That conversation birthed months of studying the Scriptures, reading some articles, and studying a couple of missional churches, which resulted in a dramatic shift in the mission committee's role within the church.

In the profile of a disciple, there are four qualities of the hand that relate to what we do as disciples. We will examine two of these qualities in this chapter and two of the qualities in the following chapter. These first two qualities pertain to living out Jesus' call on our lives to emulate His posture toward the world and make disciples of others. The following chapter will explore our commitment to using our gifts for service and being involved in the local church to build one another up in the faith.

QUALITY #5: Missional Living

The extent to which an individual understands God's mission in the world and is able to apply and replicate Jesus' posture in their own situation.

For the first two centuries in the history of the United States, the church operated out of a Christendom paradigm. This is to say that in the United States, Christianity was at the center of the culture. Denominations would open new churches in various areas, and people could often attend the church of their denominational preference and background. In the late 1970s and early 1980s, people became less loyal to a denominational preference; instead, they chose to either not go to church or go to a church that better suited their needs. This was known as the *church growth movement*, and it was built on an attractional model of ministry where churches would seek to attract people to their church through programs and styles of worship. Some good things came out of the church growth movement, but one negative repercussion was that it fed into a consumeristic culture where people would church shop and easily jump from church to church.

The other challenge with the attractional church was that it took the responsibility off individual members to share their faith and engage with their non-Christian friends. Instead, the member's responsibility was to invite people to church and let the pastor bring them to faith. Often, members didn't know non-Christians, however, because all of their friends were in the church! Even if they had non-Christian friends, most of those friendships were lost or minimized over the course of a few years as friends were replaced with people in the church.

Our culture has changed. Fewer people are looking for a church, and people are less likely to be attracted to the church. Therefore, the church—namely, those inside the church—need to go to the unchurched. This is the concept of the missional church, the sent church, the church whose members go into their surrounding context. This principle has a lot to do with an understanding of the church and its members as incarnational: Just as in Christ "the Word became flesh and dwelt among us" (John 1:14), so we are called to embody the same spirit and attitude of Jesus as we enter into our world.

There are two characteristics of missional living: understanding the ministry of Jesus and incarnational posture.

Characteristic #1: *Understanding the Ministry of Jesus*

The extent to which an individual understands Jesus' ministry in the world.

When we read the Gospels, we learn and reflect on the stories of Jesus to help us understand His nature. By concentrating on Jesus' identity, we can sometimes miss the principles that Jesus carried with Him in His ministry and how they might apply to our own lives and ministry. Do we look at how Jesus (and, for that matter, other figures in the New Testament) approached ministry opportunities differently depending upon the context? As we noted at the outset of this book, there is a great contrast between the way Jesus interacted with Nicodemus, a Pharisee, in John 3, and the way He engaged with the woman at the well in John 4. Jesus spoke with Nicodemus in a way he could understand so that the gospel made sense to him. With the woman at the well, Jesus spoke differently and connected with her given her particular situation and background. How consistently do we consider the particular needs of our friends and neighbors when we seek to speak the gospel to them?

To understand the ministry of Jesus, we also need to examine the general tone and posture that He used to approach people. Occasionally, as I walk through major cities or at public events, I see people with sandwich boards that say things like "Hell Is Hot; Turn or Burn." But when we look at the ministry of Jesus, we don't see that kind of approach to the unbelieving world. By and large, Jesus approached people in a spirit of humility and spent time asking questions to stir conversation rather than bombastically slamming people with harsh truths. True, there were times when Jesus approached with a more confrontational tone and demeanor. But these were with individuals who used their religion to put themselves above others, people whose ways and attitudes needed to be challenged.

As we understand the ministry of Jesus, we want to imagine how Jesus would approach our context. What is each person's starting place with faith? How would Jesus engage our environment? This approach isn't limited to Jesus; we see other examples in the New Testament, like in Acts, where Paul approached the religious Jewish people in a way that differed from how he approached the pagan Gentiles.

Characteristic #2: *Incarnational Posture*

The extent to which the disciple embodies the attitude and posture of Jesus in their life.

As we know, there is often a big difference between knowing what to do and actually applying that knowledge to our actions. The previous characteristic looked at the extent to which a person can understand how Jesus went about His ministries. We can derive certain principles about how Jesus approached His own ministry and can cognitively understand how we ought to go about the ministry to which God has called us. The challenge, however, comes when we ask whether *we* will apply those same characteristics to *our own ministries.*

In Philippians 2, Paul does a wonderful job describing the nature of Jesus and His posture toward the world. In verses 6 and 7, he says that "though [Jesus] was in the form of God, [he] did not count equality with God a thing to be grasped, but emptied himself, by taking the form of a servant, being born in the likeness of men." The plea that precedes this description (verse 5) is that we have the same mind that was in Christ Jesus. While Philippians 2 does a phenomenal job describing Jesus and His actions, the passage's purpose is to encourage us to *emulate* Jesus.

When we assess the quality of our discipleship, therefore, we can consider whether or not and to what extent we sacrifice for those around us. Do we sacrifice our time to serve those around us? Do we sacrifice our finances? Do we sacrifice our status and pride? Do we do these things not only for other Jesus followers or our loved ones but also for the unbelieving world around us—even those who may be hostile toward us or the gospel?

As we approach our context, do we come from a place of superiority and pride, or do we come from a posture of humility and service? Jesus expressed love and sacrifice to those from whom the religious elite would often want to keep their distance. In Matthew 19:13-15, we see that people are bringing their children to be blessed by Jesus. The disciples think that the parents are wasting Jesus' time and that these children are not important enough to see Jesus. But Jesus rebukes the disciples and instead invites the children to come to him. A similar situation is recorded in Luke 7: A woman who is described as a "sinner" comes to the Pharisee's house where Jesus is eating and begins to weep and anoint Jesus' feet with oil (verses 36-38). The Pharisee interprets Jesus' reaction—his lack of rebuke—as a sign that He is not a prophet. Jesus actually affirms the woman's actions and rebukes the Pharisee. It is responses like these that incensed the Pharisees and led them to plot Jesus' death.

Because of my denominational role, I fly a fair amount around the country. I have learned the ins and outs of airlines, and I realize that the majority of those who sit in first-class seats did not pay for those seats but got free upgrades based upon the number of miles they have flown with that particular airline (or group of airlines) the previous year. An older pastor recently informed me that airlines used to have more latitude in who they upgraded to those first-class seats. This pastor would often go to the gate agent, show his clergy card, and ask to get upgraded on a flight. I was shocked to hear that he did this but even more surprised to hear that it often worked!

I started to think hard about this pastor's actions and what must have been going through his mind. Did he really think, *Because I am a pastor and a shepherd of God's people, I shouldn't have to sit next to them on planes?* As I was engaging in my own judgment of the situation, however, the Lord was getting my attention. He was nudging me, as if to say, *Where in your life do you have the same mind-set as this pastor rather than the mind of Christ?* Unfortunately, there were significant areas in my life where an entitlement mind-set had manifested itself. And while this other pastor's self-centered mind-set was hidden from him but abundantly clear to me, I had to admit there were places in my life that hidden pride and entitlement had taken root when I was unaware.

In 1 Corinthians 13:1-3, Paul puts our gifts and talents in their proper perspective when he says,

> *If I speak in the tongues of men and of angels, but have not love, I am a noisy gong or a clanging cymbal. And if I have prophetic powers, and understand all mysteries and all knowledge, and if I have all faith, so as to remove mountains, but have not love, I am nothing. If I give away all I have, and if I deliver up my body to be burned, but have not love, I gain nothing.*

We need to pay attention to our pride. While it is important to use and develop the skills and gifts that God has given us, if we are not anchoring their use in the same sacrificial love that was present in Jesus, we may actually inadvertently do harm to the Kingdom.

QUALITY #6: Engaging Others toward Discipleship

The individual invests deeply into the lives of others to help them come to know Jesus and grow in discipleship.

In Colossians 1:28-29, Paul says that he labors with all of the energy that Christ inspires within him to present everyone mature in Christ. I have often said to congregations that I have served (and in the denomination that I lead) that our mission is to develop a greater quantity and quality of disciples. The church needs to hold both sides of that mission together. Sometimes, a church will focus heavily on reaching those who don't know Jesus in an effort to develop a greater *quantity* of disciples. Other churches might focus on "taking their people deep" to enhance the *quality* of discipleship in their church. In reality, however, both approaches are necessary, and if our churches are developing a greater quality of disciples, those disciples need to be involved in bringing new disciples to faith and helping them grow in their maturity as well. There are therefore two characteristics embedded in this quality. The first has to do with reaching new people for Jesus, and the second involves encouraging other disciples to deepen their relationship with the Lord.

Characteristic #1: *Helping nonbelievers come to know the Lord*

The extent to which an individual effectively connects and communicates with those who are not yet Christian.

Helping those who do not yet know the Lord put their faith in Jesus is a challenging task, especially in our post-Christian culture. In this day and age, society often believes that religion is a matter of preference rather than truth, just like choosing a hairstyle is a matter of personal preference rather than a matter of "right" or "wrong." Religion is often seen through a lens of choosing what works for you as an individual or a family. This perspective is further complicated by the feeling that Christianity is often seen as judgmental, and being non-judgmental is one of the highest values in our society.

A Christian's task, therefore, is complicated and involves first earning the right to be heard by others. When I was first trained in evangelism, I was using the *Four Spiritual Laws* from Campus Crusade for Christ (now Cru). We were encouraged to initiate conversations with strangers and steer the conversation toward the good news that God loves them and has a wonderful plan for their life. I like this means of explaining how God relates to people and will often use these concepts as I dig deeper into faith conversations. The *Four Spiritual Laws* presume the reality of universal truths, and the people I was sharing them with seemed to agree with that concept. As time progressed, however, people were more and more put off by being approached outside the context of relationship. They didn't respond to a generic presentation of the gospel; they would only tolerate religious conversations that occurred in the context of relationship.

Therefore, much more time had to be spent developing these relationships. They needed to be developed not only to eventually share the gospel but also to display the love of Jesus. This characteristic seeks to consider the way in which the disciple is developing these kinds of relationships. Do those who don't yet know Jesus understand that the disciple honestly cares for them as opposed to considering them a project? Does the disciple listen to the questions and objections that someone raises? Does the disciple relate the gospel in a way that is meaningful and pertinent to those who don't know the Lord? Does the disciple allow the nonbeliever to come to faith at an appropriate pace rather than trying to needlessly hurry the process?[1]

On the other end of the spectrum is the tendency to shy away from sharing our faith with others. I see this as the more frequent approach rather than rushing the evangelism process or making a one-size-fits-all process. Usually, our fear is that if we share our faith, it will be rejected, and in the process, our friendship will be hindered. Therefore, the normal course of action is to refrain from sharing our faith with others unless those individuals practically beg us to tell them about Jesus.

This characteristic, then, often takes a lot of work to strengthen. Not only do we need to have the inner heart conviction that we need to share our faith but we also need to focus on how we can develop relationships that lead to sharing our faith. We need to learn how to ask good questions. We need to learn how to understand the underlying thought processes, assumptions, and needs of those with whom we have relationship. Finally, we need to learn the right balance in sharing our faith at an appropriate pace that facilitates the process of people putting their faith and trust in Jesus.

Characteristic #2: *Engaging Believers toward Discipleship*

The extent to which the individual works with other believers to help them become mature disciples.

Frequently, congregations will identify their goal to "make disciples who make disciples" in their mission statement. The point is that they don't just want to make disciples; they want to support a process by which the disciples they make are reproducing their discipleship in other people. This is an important value, but it is also a little redundant. Scripture is clear that the responsibility to develop the quantity and quality of disciples is in the very DNA of a disciple.

The challenge is that often, our churches do not create the infrastructure or the expectation that disciples are to make other disciples. Individuals that *are* engaged in making disciples of others are usually the exception, not the rule. I remember recognizing this disconnect in the church I was pastoring. I was approached by a younger believer in his late twenties who asked if I could connect him with someone to disciple him. He wanted someone who had raised kids and who also had a strong marriage and a deep faith. I immediately thought of one of my elders, Dave.

Dave had a mature faith that had been especially deepened in the last few years. He had a great relationship with his wife and with his two daughters, both believers who were finishing college. Dave had the type of family that young men want to have when they grow up.

I approached Dave to ask him if he might meet with this young man and help him grow as a disciple. Dave desperately wanted to meet this challenge, but he admitted, "I have no idea how to disciple other people," so Dave and I met so that I could prepare him to disciple someone else. We continued to meet and debrief as he reflected on his experiences fostering the faith of this young man. In the end, everything worked out very well. The young man grew in his faith and in the maturity of his relationships. Dave gained a new skill to help others become strong disciples and was passionate about continuing those types of relationships in the future.

What I realized in that experience is that it wasn't Dave's fault for not knowing how to disciple other people initially. It was my responsibility to set the expectation that helping others mature in faith was normal in the Christian life. I knew that if I expected other people to engage in life-on-life discipleship, then I needed to model the practice.

In order to be an effective disciple maker, a person needs to have not only a clear picture of what a disciple is but also the skill and commitment to engage with others in deep relationships. These relationships require trust that leads to transparency and authenticity. The mentor needs to be able to pinpoint places of health and opportunities for growth with those that they are discipling and help them develop in those areas.

In this chapter, we talked about two qualities of the hand that are associated with living out our faith. These two qualities relate to the way we engage in the contexts where God has placed us to develop the quantity and quality of disciples of Jesus Christ. In the next chapter, we will look at the final two qualities associated with the actions of our faith: how we live out our discipleship within the local congregation and how we utilize our God-given gifts.

REFLECTION QUESTIONS

1. What do you notice about the way Jesus interacted with people? How did He interact with religious people as compared to nonreligious people?

2. What can we learn from Jesus' attitude as we engage with the world around us?

3. Who has helped you grow in your faith? How was that person influential?

4. Who has God put in your path who is not a Christian? How might God use you to bring them to faith?

5. Who are newer or younger believers that you might help to grow up in the faith?

CHAPTER 7

Qualities of the Hand, Part 2

The Ministry of a Disciple

PASTOR BOB ANNOUNCED that the church was going to do a congregation-wide study on discerning your call and purpose to serve both inside and outside the church. The church had recently assessed the congregation and found that only 15 percent of its members were serving. When Pastor Bob looked at the numbers, he was also concerned that more than half of those that were serving were doing needed things but not in a way that used a discernible spiritual gift. He was also disappointed that by and large the people in the church didn't have significant friendships with nonbelievers.

Pastor Bob laid out the plan for this eight-week, church-wide study. The church was going to stop all other activities.

Everyone was encouraged to get into a small group to go through the material. They were going to discover their spiritual gifts and how God had shaped them to partner with Him in the world. The process would end with each person working with a trained individual to find opportunities for them to serve within and outside the church.

This church-wide program received mixed reviews. Some members were happy to discover their purpose, but some comments indicated a less-than-favorable response. Some made comments like "Why should we do more around the church? Isn't that what we pay the staff to do?" People said this in a joking spirit, but you could tell that they spoke honestly. Others said that they had put in their time serving or that they couldn't serve at this stage in their lives. Some indicated that they felt trying to engage their non-Christian neighbors would not be taken well, plus they didn't think they had the gift of evangelism. Pastor Bob knew that the next eight weeks and beyond were going to be an uphill battle.

In the last chapter, we talked about taking the posture of Jesus toward our world and replicating His mission of evangelism, discipleship, justice, and mercy within our own contexts. In this chapter, we will look at the final two qualities of discipleship, which pertain to living out our commitment to Jesus Christ utilizing the gifts that He has given us within and beyond our local expression of the body of Christ.

QUALITY #7: Community

The extent to which the individual is living out the call to be engaged in a local expression of the body of Christ.

God did not create us to live the Christian life in isolation from other believers; rather, all through the New Testament, we see Christians gathering together to worship the Lord, build one another up, and serve God's mission in the world. The author of Hebrews speaks powerful words about resisting the temptation to withdraw from Christian community in chapter 10 (verses 24-25):

> *And let us consider how to stir up one another to love and good works, not neglecting to meet together, as is the habit of some, but encouraging one another, and all the more as you see the Day drawing near.*

There are two characteristics within the quality of community: local congregation commitment and deeper Christian community.

Characteristic #1: Local Congregation Commitment

The extent to which an individual is committed to the mission and ministry of a local church.

Several factors contribute to self-identifying Christians not considering involvement in a local church a necessary part of practicing their faith. For one thing, our society has often focused on the importance of the individual above the needs of the community. According to this perspective, the community is only important insomuch as it enhances the life of the individual. Therefore, people look at the local churches, weigh the benefits and costs of membership, and determine individually whether or not it is worth it to join one.

This is further exacerbated by churches posturing themselves as able to meet the needs of those who attend. When a church seeks to "sell" themselves based on the way the programs they offer meet the needs of their congregants, then the congregants will leave as soon as the programs are not sufficiently meeting their needs.

We also see times when the local church has hurt or damaged others. Maybe there has been sexual, physical, or verbal abuse by a leader or other member. In these cases, individuals may be hesitant to trust the church again and seek instead to develop their faith on their own.

But the local church is not optional in Jesus' plan for believers. The local church is to be both a gift and a responsibility for the individual Christian. The end of Ephesians 4 gives a great picture of a mature congregation. This congregation is solidly committed to the truth of the gospel. It is tightly joined together as a body, and each part of the body is doing its part within the body to build the others up. It is a beautiful picture of the body of Christ as well as the necessity and importance of each member.

Assessing our local-church commitment involves looking at how we utilize our resources (such as time, money, and spiritual gifts) to fulfill the larger vision of the congregation. When I was a local-church pastor, I wanted to take time in public worship to acknowledge when people chose to officially join the body. Individuals would affirm or reaffirm their faith, as well as commit to using their gifts and talents to build up the body of Christ and support our God-given mission. The current church members would also commit to building up the new members via discipleship. It was a short but beautiful time to reinforce God's desire for the church.

In this category, a disciple's health is also related to that person's willingness to submit to the church's leadership. The real test of disciples in the life of the church is how they respond when the church goes in a direction with which they disagree. Assuming the church isn't doing something wrong (such as changing core theology, mishandling funds, or covering up predatory behavior), is the disciple willing to support the church's leadership and direction? Hebrews 13:17 tells disciples,

Obey your leaders and submit to them, for they are keeping watch over your souls, as those who will have to give an account. Let them do this with joy and not with groaning, for that would be of no advantage to you.

Characteristic #2: *Deeper Christian Community*

The extent to which the individual belongs to a smaller group of believers with whom they serve and grow.

There are some aspects of biblical Christian community that cannot be fully lived out in the context of an entire church but are better pursued among a smaller group of believers. For example, Hebrews 10:24-25 tells us that the Christian community is to spur one another on to love and good deeds. This does happen within the context of corporate worship, where the preacher seeks to fulfill this duty within the context of the sermon. In order for the Christian community to truly do this for one another, however, this task needs to be undertaken in a smaller, more intimate context.

This characteristic asks if the individual is part of a small group of individuals within the larger Christian community who are consistently committed to one another's discipleship. This group doesn't need to be a formal small group; it could also be a missional community or a prayer covenant group. The point is whether the disciple has a smaller community where they are known at a deeper and more intimate level than is likely to occur within an established church context. Is the disciple part of a group that knows them at a deeper level, part of an environment in which they can speak the truth in love to one another?

Sometimes even small groups don't have these characteristics and are merely smaller groups of individuals who study the Bible together but do not really encourage or love one another at that more intimate level. I worked with a church that was trying to revitalize and enhance its small-group ministry. Church members said that what prompted their need to do so was that when one couple got a divorce, their small-group members were surprised—they hadn't even known the couple was having problems. Another couple who was dating had moved in together, and no one in their small group knew. Finally—and most tragically—a man in a small group took his own life; no one had known that he was experiencing depression. Simply being in a small group is not sufficient. Group members need to display a level of authenticity and transparency with one another.

Some churches (such as house churches) are small enough and interconnected enough that they can fulfill both the corporate worship functions of a church and the mutual encouragement of these smaller gatherings. In these situations, it is important that the house church is careful not to neglect the full function of church. Individuals that plan this type of gathering need to ensure that there is a communal purpose beyond the gathering itself, and that the members understand and apply their gifts in fulfillment of the full life of a disciple.

QUALITY #8: Fulfilling God's Call on Their Life

The extent to which an individual understands, develops, and utilizes the gifts that God has given them and lives into their call.

When I finished seminary and began pastoring my first church, I was twenty-five years old. The average age of the congregation I served was about seventy-two! These were a great group of saints that loved the Lord and were willing to do anything to help the church. For a couple of years, guys in their seventies would mow three acres of grass, climb trees to trim them, and clean gutters on the roof. The property looked better than that of any church I had seen that didn't have professional landscapers. In my second year at the church, I led a series of Bible studies on discovering your spiritual gifts. An older gentleman in the church named Harold said to me, "I see what you are trying to do, Dana—you are trying to make us all ministers."

I was a little concerned about the tone with which he approached the question. Harold followed, however, by saying, "I have done a lot of things around this church. I built these cabinets, and I have put in sprinklers, but no one ever told me I could be a minister." He concluded with tears in his eyes and a crack in his voice, "I think I might have some gifts that went unused."

I assured Harold that the things he had done around the church were extremely valuable and needed. But I also assured him that it wasn't too late to start serving out of his particular giftedness. Harold got involved in a mentoring program that met at our church. He started tutoring and mentoring a ten-year-old boy, beginning a relationship that went on for several years. This boy, Andy, had no father his entire life. Harold shared the gospel with his words and actions, and Andy gave his life to Jesus.

Harold came alive! He still did a number of things around the church but was also able to utilize his spiritual gifts for God's mission in the world. As I watched Harold serve, I realized that there were two benefits to fulfilling the call on our lives.

First, we get to see and participate in the Kingdom of God on earth.

Second, we experience immeasurable joy when we utilize the gifts that God has given to us and participate in the ministry for which He has created us.

In this last quality, we look at two different characteristics related to fulfilling the call on our lives. First is discerning and confirming the gifts for which we have been created. Second is our ability to grow in utilizing our own and others' gifts and skills for ministry.

Characteristic #1: *Understanding of Gifts, Roles, and Calling*

The extent to which an individual understands their spiritual gifts and utilizes those gifts in God's call upon their life.

As members serve in the life of the congregation, there are certain activities that require people to serve in ways that are not related to their spiritual gifts. For example, after an event, we may need people to help stack chairs, take out the trash, and so on. I haven't read any spiritual-gifts assessment that includes the gift of stacking chairs, though this skill might be related to hospitality. We need to do these things, however; they are an inherent part of being actively involved in life together as a congregation. The challenge is that—like my friend Harold—we may only serve in these ways and not utilize the gifts that God has given us to engage in His mission in the world.

It is not the purpose of this book to take positions about which spiritual gifts are or are not active today but rather to affirm the common agreement that God has uniquely gifted and called each one of us to ministry. I love the concept in Ephesians 2: While we have been saved by grace and not by works, God has still prepared in advance good works for us to do.

One of the mentors in my life is Bob Logan, who trained me as a coach and has been influential in my own understanding of discipleship. Bob gave me the greatest definition of success, which he obtained from his father, Sam Logan: *finding out what God wants you to do and doing it.* I love this definition because we can't compare ourselves to the accomplishments of other people. Our task as disciples is to discover the good works God has prepared for us in advance and pursue those works.

Once Harold realized that he was called to minister to people, we sat down and talked about his gifts, experiences, personality, and passions. Harold had an extremely patient and pleasant personality; he also had high expectations for others. He had lived in the community for fifty years and saw it experience rapid changes. He saw the decreasing number of people following Jesus and the higher and higher number of students who didn't have fathers. Harold's wife, who had passed away, had been an educator in the schools, and Harold was passionate about education. It was clear to me that his personality and passion would be perfect for mentoring students, and it was great to see what occurred over the ensuing two years with Andy. Both their lives were changed, and Harold's renewed sense of purpose and joy from partnering with God for His purposes in the world showed other members of the congregation how they could participate in wider aspects of ministry through the church.

Some aspects of our gifts and calling may be best realized within the ministries of the local church. But our calling from God also extends beyond the church into the larger world we live in. As churches, we want to be careful that we don't pigeonhole people into a ministry exclusive to the church, failing to honor the holistic call in a person's life. I know I have been guilty of validating service that occurred in our established ministries rather than helping people see how they were using their gifts and callings in their secular vocations, schools, neighborhoods, and other venues.

Characteristic #2: *Growing in Ministry Skill*

The extent to which an individual is proactive in growing their ability to do ministry.

In Santa Barbara, where I grew up, there were three public high schools. Every year, the local Toyota dealer gave away a brand-new car to a senior from one of these schools. Each school had an after-prom party and drew five names who would have a chance at the car. I was one of the five from my school who had that chance. Then, on the Monday after the last school had their prom, the five students from each school went down to the dealership and there was a reverse drawing for the car. A reverse drawing meant that the last person whose name was drawn won the car. People's names were drawn, and they won various cash prizes. There were two names left in the hat: my name and that of a friend of mine from my high school. His name got pulled, he won $200, and I won a brand-new Toyota Tercel.

I was thrilled! The local news was there; some of my friends were there. The news crew wanted to get a picture of me driving the car out of the show room. I got in the car, strapped on my seat belt, and realized that the car was a stick shift! I didn't know how to drive a stick shift, so the news crew stopped rolling film, and eventually, my mom had to drive the car home with me in the passenger's seat. I then had to spend a week learning to drive my new car in the parking lot of a school near my house before I was allowed to take it on the road.

The point is that I had been given this wonderful gift, but I didn't know how to use it. The same can be true for us as disciples. We have been created to play great roles for God's purposes, but we may not yet know how to fulfill those roles. Initial and ongoing training can teach us how to use and maximize our skills to advance God's Kingdom.

Growing in ministry skill is a continuation of discovering our gifts and living into the call that God has given us. In the simple discipleship assessment, questions about growing in ministry skill encourage Christ followers to discern their unique gifts and—importantly—identify areas for potential growth. For example, a new small-group leader might be gifted at nurturing a community of mutual care and support for spiritual growth, but that leader may need to grow in their ability to facilitate discussion or deal with challenging members. A more experienced small-group leader might have these skills down pretty well but might need to strengthen their ability to raise new leaders.

The challenge that many of our churches face is that we haven't identified the skills that people need in various ministries of the church. As a result, training is often either nonexistent or so generic that it doesn't address the specific task at hand.

Growing in ministry skill isn't just about awareness, though. It's also about a person's willingness to engage in challenging growth opportunities. Often, we only engage in ministry tasks when we feel comfortable; therefore, we see people relying on their own ability rather than tapping into the Lord's power. It is only when we are stretched beyond our natural ability that we are really able to trust the Lord and grow beyond our capacity.

A theme we continually see in Scripture is that God doesn't call the equipped; He equips the called. God doesn't delegate ministry to the person with the best résumé for the task, knowing that disciple can handle the job so that He can move on to other things. Instead, what we see throughout Scripture is that when people say *yes* to challenging assignments, then the Lord equips them for their tasks. There are many, many examples of this practice in Scripture; one obvious one is Moses. In Exodus chapter 3, Moses gives God a list of reasons why he is not qualified to do the task that God is seeking to give him. God assures Moses that He will go with him, and that his success will be based not upon his own ability but on God's power and strength.

This is the nature of mature discipleship: willingness to trust God with our gifts and to follow where He leads—into greater impact and greater joy.

REFLECTION QUESTIONS

1. How would you respond to someone who said, "You don't have to go to church to be a Christian"?

2. With whom do you have a relationship that encourages depth and transparency? If it is hard to identify people that fit this category, with which acquaintances might you develop deeper relationships?

3. Why is having a few deep relationships so important to spiritual growth, and what are the challenges to having these relationships?

4. What gifts, skills, and passions has God given you to serve His purpose?

5. In what ways can you grow in your ability to serve Him?

CHAPTER 8

Designing a Personal Plan for Discipleship

IN A VISIONING PROCESS for the future, the staff at Elevate Church wanted to create a leadership development pipeline. Their goal was to have a clear plan to lead nonbelievers to the Lord and see those new believers mature in their faith, thereby creating a farm system from which to recruit future leaders. Everyone bought into the concept. The disagreement erupted, however, over how this pipeline would work.

One member of the staff, Tom, wanted to make a series of classes that people could go through systematically to get the education they needed. His argument was that this was the most efficient way, given their weekend worship averaged five thousand members. Tom said, "People love the Wednesday night classes that we offer; let's make that into a more formal academy."

Another staff member, Kate, who had a campus-ministry background, argued that growth doesn't happen in a classroom. She contended that the approach needed to be more individualized. Her idea was immediately rejected by several members of the staff. They thought that while Kate's idea would be great in a smaller church or setting, it would be unrealistic to implement in such a large church. One staff member said, "Kate, your idea is noble, but how are we going to create individual plans for so many people? How can we even find enough qualified people to work with every member of the congregation?"

The above challenge plays out in many congregational settings. We know that people grow best through personalized approaches, and yet the perceived obstacles to helping people grow on a case-by-case basis seem enormous. In addition, because churches tend to approach ministry programmatically, congregants and staff tend to approach solutions from the same perspective. The goal of this chapter and the next is to alleviate these fears and see that taking a personalized approach to discipleship is possible, effective, and actually less labor intensive than running programs.

This chapter will focus on how to develop a personalized plan for discipleship. The following three chapters will focus on how those involved in the discipleship of others—such as mentors, one-on-one disciple makers, triads, covenant groups, and small groups—can help in this process.

ASSESSING YOUR ASSESSMENT

The first step in developing a personalized plan for discipleship is to assess your current state of discipleship. This involves an honest measure of the qualities and characteristics of a disciple as they are exhibited in your life. The simple discipleship assessment was developed as an efficient means for measuring these qualities and characteristics.

The first section looks at the health of the eight core qualities of a disciple. The second breaks those scores down into the health of the twenty-one supporting characteristics. Each of these qualities is shown on a bar graph and ranked on a scale from 1 to 5. Five is the highest level of health, and a 1 is the lowest level of health. You will notice when you take the online assessment that your score is on the top in blue, and the observer score is below in orange. Take a quick look at which of your qualities and characteristics are high and which ones are lower. In the second section of the assessment, you will see the results connected to the qualities and characteristics that are measured.

It is important to mention that even though the assessment has gone through a rigorous statistical validation process, the lowest score on your assessment isn't necessarily the area that you should work on the most for your discipleship. The assessment is meant to help you figure out—with the Lord and others—the area(s) that need focused attention. As you look at the numbers and comments from your friends and process them in your community with the Lord's leading, the direction suggested by the discipleship plan will become clear.

The first time I took the assessment, there were two areas

that the Lord brought together to help me determine where I
needed to grow. The first area had to do with satisfied living,
which is related to a spirit of peace, joy, and patience. I knew
that I can often be impatient and sometimes a little tense, so
I rated myself a little lower in the items associated with this
characteristic. My observers, some of whom were family and
coworkers, rated me even a little lower! They saw me as even
more impatient than I saw myself.

I also saw that some of the items related to the quality of a
gospel-saturated life were a little low. I tend to want to take my
identity from what I do rather than from who I am, a beloved
child of God. My joy can sometimes be contingent upon the success of my ministry or how others perceive my performance.

As I prayed over my results and talked with my community
about what the results were telling me, I saw a relationship
between the two areas for improvement. I was often impatient
because I wanted to produce more to please God and others.
Therefore, my lower score in the satisfied-living characteristic
was really a symptom of the deeper issue related to a gospel-
centered identity. While "satisfied living" rated a lower score on
the assessment, the area that I was called to work on was taking
my identity from who I was in the Lord, not my success or failure.

DETERMINE A CLEAR OUTCOME

The second step in the process of developing a personal plan
for discipleship is to understand and articulate a clear goal for
the future. Once you have determined the general area where
you want to grow, it is important to gain clarity on what type
of growth you would like to see. If, for example, you want to

have a great understanding of the Trinity, then you will want to present a picture of what you hope will be true about your knowledge of the Trinity after you have completed your plan. So an illustration of a clear goal would be "By December 1, I want to be able to articulate the nature of the Trinity to new Christians in such a way that they will comprehend what I am saying." If you want to grow in your prayer life, then a goal might be "By March 30, I will be praying at least twice a day for fifteen minutes, and at least half of that time will involve listening for God's leading."

Notice in these steps that the disciple needs to articulate a clear picture of the future within a particular timeframe. This allows the creation of a particular target, an end point when you will assess your progress. How far into the future should this end point be? We need to have the right balance of enough time to make significant progress while not setting the timeframe so far into the future that your design could get a little bit stale or you could get sidetracked by other priorities. If you have a goal that will take longer than three to four months, then it is probably wise to make the goal smaller and more manageable, so that you can see some progress in a three- to four-month period. I often find that if the goal is longer than three to four months, the plan will involve some significant reshaping anyway, so three to four months provides a good time for reevaluation.

DEVELOP YOUR PLAN FOR GROWTH

Once we determine the area where the Lord has called us to grow, we need to develop a plan for discipleship. As we develop these plans, we must do so in a way that is consistent with how Jesus made disciples (see chapter 2). For example, Jesus did more than just give information to His disciples; He also led people into experiences that solidified the truth and caused them to grow.

Another fact about Jesus' discipleship is that He understood true growth takes time and intentional effort. My experience finding my identity in the gospel rather than accomplishments is a perfect example: Simply having more information about who I was in Christ wasn't going to bring transformation. My approach was going to have to be holistic and intentional, and it was going to take time.

The model for approaching growth as a disciple in this book is greatly influenced by the work of Malcolm Webber, the executive director of LeaderSource SGA. Malcolm's approach to helping people grow is very simple and yet very profound. He asks individuals to develop and commit to opportunities around four different dimensions, or what he calls 4Ds.[1] These four dimensions are engaging with God, engaging with truth, engaging with community, and engaging with experience. When we create a well-balanced set of activities in these four areas, Webber suggests, over a period of time we will have a much greater chance of experiencing growth in our discipleship and leadership.

Webber's model of developing a plan to grow as a disciple is so simple that I have used it with my eight-year-old daughter as well as those who have been pastors for thirty years. The way I help people think of these four different types of activities that they need to incorporate is to think about four different directions. I use the following diagram to help illustrate these directions:

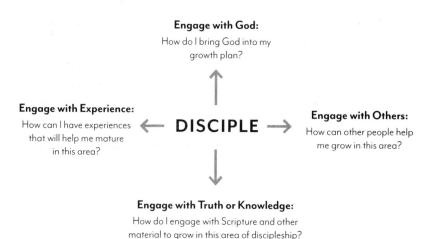

Engage with God:
How do I bring God into my
growth plan?

Engage with Experience:
How can I have experiences
that will help me mature
in this area?

← **DISCIPLE** →

Engage with Others:
How can other people help
me grow in this area?

Engage with Truth or Knowledge:
How do I engage with Scripture and other
material to grow in this area of discipleship?

ENGAGE WITH GOD: The First Direction

The first direction that we need to engage is with God. This probably seems relatively obvious, and yet it is easy for us to forget to make this facet of our growth plan particularly robust. Especially if our area of growth relates to growing in knowledge or ministry skills, it can be tempting to leave this aspect out of our development plan.

The basic question in this facet of our plan is *How do we bring the Lord into our development plan?* If we want to grow in areas related to our hearts (the first characteristics), then we might want to ask what spiritual disciplines we want to engage. In developing my plan for growth in living out my identity as a follower of Jesus, I went on a daylong silent retreat where I journaled and prayed for the Lord to show me the places in my life where I was not living out of my own sonship of Jesus. I also committed to the spiritual practice of a daily examen: At two scheduled times, I asked God how I had been doing living out of my adoption as a child of God. This discipline of regularly stopping activity and asking God to examine my heart was extremely helpful to keep my discipleship design at the forefront of my mind, especially since I can be impatient, and pausing to reflect doesn't always come naturally to me. I also daily asked the Lord to help me to live out the details of my design. I knew that there would be other things that could easily derail me from fulfilling my discipleship plan, and I needed God's help to persevere.

The key in this area is to find ways to engage with the Lord that will specifically address your design. Some general activities can be useful to all types of designs, such as praying for God's help. Other activities are particularly helpful to address specific qualities and characteristics. For example, if someone wants to grow in the characteristic of devoted living, which is related to faithfulness and self-control in the fruit of the Spirit, that person may want to fast, as that is particularly related to having the Spirit of God help control our appetites.

If a disciple wants to grow in one of the qualities related to the hands (i.e., what we do for the Lord), then they will want to engage with God in ways that are specific to those particular needs and focus. For example, a person may want to grow in their ability to disciple a new believer. Ironically, it could be easy to leave God out of the equation. The temptation could be simply to read books about discipleship and try to apply the information contained in those books to particular situations.

But we want to make sure that our plan for growth as a disciple in this area includes engaging with God. This person could also take a retreat to ask God how He has formed that person as a disciple, since it is often easy for us to forget that God has led us on our individual journeys.

If a disciple wants to grow in areas related to increasing knowledge, then perhaps in addition to asking God for the ability to stick to their plan, they may also want to ask God to reveal His truth. Several passages remind us that we can't obtain truth apart from God. Passages like John 16:13, which says, "When the Spirit of truth comes, he will guide you into all the truth, for he will not speak on his own authority, but whatever he hears he will speak, and he will declare to you the things that are to come." Paul also reminds us that we need the Spirit of God to understand truth. In 1 Corinthians 2:12, he says, "Now we have received not the spirit of the world, but the Spirit who is from God, that we might understand the things freely given us by God."

ENGAGE WITH TRUTH OR KNOWLEDGE:
The Second Direction

On the other side of the diagram, we see the need to engage with truth or knowledge. The most obvious form of knowledge that we need to engage in is connecting with God's Word. It is particularly helpful to consider how we will engage with God's Word as it relates to the needs presented in our design.

When I wanted to increase my ability to take my iden-tity from my position in the Lord, I decided to try reading the Gospels through the lens of how an individual's identity in Christ changes his or her attitude and actions. As I read through the Gospels asking this question, it added a component to these stories that I had not experienced before.

For example, I read Luke 18 and encountered a wealthy man who asks Jesus how to inherit eternal life. Jesus is unusually combative with him: "Why do you call me good?" He asks, in what I imagine to be a testy tone (verse 19). Jesus invites the ruler to obey five of the Ten Commandments—those associated with how we live among other people. The ruler asserts his righteousness, which Jesus counters by confronting the man's attachment to his wealth—the sixth social commandment. As the ruler abandons Jesus, Jesus points out the problem of a works-based righteousness: There's always something we stop short of doing, something we love that we won't surrender to God.

And then I turned to Luke 19, where I met another wealthy man, Zacchaeus. Universally derided as a sinner, Zacchaeus does nothing to argue his case to Jesus. He doesn't even introduce himself to Jesus—Jesus introduces himself to Zacchaeus! And while the ruler in Luke 18 refuses Jesus' invitation to divest himself of his idol (wealth), Zacchaeus responds to Jesus' kindness by replacing his idolatry of money with an eagerness to learn about Jesus and His Kingdom!

Turning back to Luke 18, I noticed that shortly before his encounter with the ruler, Jesus tells a parable about a righteous man and a tax collector in which the righteous man leaves the Temple without the peace of God, but the tax collector—the sinner—goes home justified before God! Stripped of our idols, I learned from these stories, we discover grace.

As we engage with knowledge, we not only want to connect

with Scripture but we may also want to tap into other types of information. There may be particular books, articles, podcasts, and so on that are helpful for your particular area of growth. For my initial plan, I had two books that were part of my reading. I read all of one of the books, and I reread a chapter from John Ortberg's book about the life you've always wanted called "An Unhurried Life," which was extremely helpful in looking at my own patience.[2]

If you want to grow in particular skills for ministry, you may want to read study guides or manuals about pertinent topics. I once worked with someone who wanted to better understand and apply their spiritual gifts. They found a course that included audio and video lectures about spiritual gifts. They also engaged in a spiritual-gifts assessment and some material to unpack their findings.

The great and challenging thing is that we live in the information age, which means that many helpful resources are available to enrich our discipleship plans. It also means that we can get overwhelmed by the amount of resources and the task of determining their quality. As we develop our plans, it is important that we do so in conjunction with others. Other individuals and the leadership of our larger church communities can help make sure that we find the appropriate resources to aid in our development. This brings us to the third direction we need to experience: engage with others.

ENGAGE WITH OTHERS: The Third Direction

It is important that we involve the greater community around us as we engage in discipleship. Especially for introverts, it is easy to simply include God and personal study in our discipleship journey—without involving others in the process. But God has given us the great gift of the church. These other believers encourage us and use their gifts to help us become mature disciples of Jesus.

Two of the churches I served celebrated Communion by distributing the elements separately. The tray of bread would come around, and people would take one, and then later, the tray with small cups of grape juice would be passed. In these churches, I would have people take the bread on their own timing after prayer and reflection, to get across the fact that we all need to come to Jesus individually. We are not Christians because our parents were Christians; we need to confess our sins and faith as individuals. The cups, however, we held until everyone had received one, and then the entire congregation took the element at the same time. This was done to symbolize the fact that when we are saved, we are saved into the larger body of Christ.

The question in this third direction is how other people participate in our personalized plan for discipleship. In some cases, we may want to ask individuals who know us well to give us feedback in a particular area. For example, since I often struggle with patience, one of the things that I did was ask my kids to point out when they sensed that I wasn't giving them my full attention.

We can also involve other people by asking them to pray for our discipleship design or to keep us accountable to it. We might, therefore, choose two to five people to share our design with, and then have weekly check-ins to identify progress and address challenges together.

ENGAGE WITH EXPERIENCE: The Fourth Direction

When Jesus encouraged others toward discipleship, He would give them tasks that let them apply what they were learning but also became opportunities to reflect and refine their thinking. I think of the saying "You don't learn how to swim in a classroom" as helpful for this aspect of our growth. This makes perfect sense, doesn't it? The classroom can give you some information. In the classroom, an instructor can show you videos of other people swimming so you can observe and dissect the mechanics of their stroke. The instructor can also provide critical feedback about your own stroke. But the real way you learn how to swim is by getting into the pool and swimming.

We therefore need to ask what experiences we might create for ourselves to stimulate growth in a particular area. If we need to grow in areas of the heart, then we will want to engage in particular experiences that help us in this area. This reminds me of someone I work with who wanted to grow in sacrificial living. They felt they were pretty stingy in their use of money and time with others. The best way they could grow was by practicing sacrificially giving of themselves for the sake of others; therefore, they decided to begin regularly giving away a greater percentage of their finances than before. They also decided on practical ways to redistribute their time sacrificially to serve others. This experience was very helpful in breaking them of the self-centered mentality that humans frequently display.

If someone wants to grow in the area of knowledge, then they may want to develop some experiences to help ensure that they gain the knowledge they are looking for. For example, if someone wants to grow in knowledge of the New Testament, then they may want to find an opportunity to share what they know already with a younger or newer believer. They may want to write a paper on some aspect of the New Testament they feel particular passion about, have someone ask them questions, or take an online test.

The most obvious need for experiences come in the area of developing skills and abilities—the qualities of the hand. I worked with a person who wanted to be able to disciple other believers. It makes sense that in order to grow in our ability to disciple others, we actually need to practice discipling others. They identified two people that they were going to meet with to help them grow as disciples. In the category of community, they put as part of their activity to meet with me twice a month to reflect and debrief their discipleship experiences.

In creating these discipleship plans, we want to avoid approaching them as a formula to grow as a disciple. Our growth as disciples is not formulaic; instead, these four directions help us ask the right questions to address our desire to grow as disciples. Creating these can be both fun and challenging. It is challenging to try to think of how best to design my own growth, but I find that when people develop this type of plan, they are excited and eagerly anticipate what the Lord is going to do.

Hopefully by this time you have some idea of where you might want to grow as a disciple. Perhaps you have multiple possibilities. Pick one and make a practice design, asking yourself the basic questions below. (You may also want to consult appendix C for example designs.)

REFLECTION QUESTIONS

1. How do you need to involve God in this design?

2. What Scripture might you want to study or reflect on?

3. What other material might you want to read, listen to, or study?

4. In what ways can you involve others to help you grow?

5. What practical experiences might you engage in to help you grow?

CHAPTER 9

Discipling as Coaching

SHARI WAS A LITTLE NERVOUS. Now a fifty-eight-year-old woman, Shari had been raised in the church. She became a Christian in her parents' church and had been actively involved in church for her whole life. Her pastor had just asked Shari to engage in a discipling relationship with Emily, a woman who had recently joined their church. Emily was a relatively new mother who desperately wanted her family to have a Christian foundation. The pastor thought that the best course of action would be to connect Emily with a more mature believer who had already raised their kids to adulthood. Shari seemed like a natural choice.

Shari was willing to take on the task of discipling Emily,

but was not sure if she could do so effectively. All kinds of questions ran through Shari's head:

Where do I start?

What should I tell her to do?

What if she doesn't want to do what I suggest?

What if I give her bad advice?

What if I don't have the answers she is looking for?

What if she needs resources that I can't provide?

Shari's questions are natural questions; in fact, I would be a little concerned if someone new to a discipling relationship didn't have some reservations about helping people grow in their discipleship. However, some of Shari's concerns might be alleviated if she viewed herself more as Emily's coach than as her mentor.

WHAT IS COACHING?

We typically think of discipleship relationships in the category of mentoring. A mentoring relationship is where someone who has more experience or knowledge seeks to transfer that information to someone younger or less mature. One person, the mentor, sets the agenda and the content for the relationship. The person being mentored either seeks out the mentor or is assigned a mentor with the hopes that they will become like the mentor. Sometimes the idea of a *mentor* is one who is "above" or has gone before the other person and pours into that other person.

The image of a coach is different. A *coach* is alongside the person and draws out of the other person. While the analogy of a sports coach has its limitations, it can also be very helpful in trying to understand how a coach might function in helping another person grow in the area of discipleship.

Think of any professional athlete, such as a tennis player. The tennis player has a coach that conducts her training. The coach is likely not a better tennis player than the person she is coaching; otherwise, she would be playing on the professional circuit herself. Even if the coach previously played professionally, she may not have been a world-class player. Consequently, the coach does not try to replicate herself in the player. Rather, the coach comes alongside the player, drawing out the best in her so she can compete at the highest level.

Coaches are not only used in sports. There are also, for example, coaches in business. Business executives have been meeting with coaches for years, and it is becoming more and more of a common practice to pair middle- and even entry-level managers with a coach. Oftentimes, executive coaches are not experts in the various fields they coach, but they create an environment that allows clients to think strategically about short- and long-term goals.

Coaching has gained in popularity; as a result, this craft is increasingly practiced. It is not an officially regulated practice, but everything seems to be going in that direction. The gold standard for defining coaching and certifying coaches is the International Coach Federation (ICF). The ICF has different levels of certification, each of which involves required hours of training, mentoring, and practical experience. This organization articulates eleven coaching competencies and levels of proficiency within each competency for certification. I am an ICF-certified coach and have found it one of the most valuable skills that I possess.

The intention of this book is not to make you a professional coach but to give you a simple understanding of coaching, so that you can apply it in your discipleship relationship. The coach does several things to help the person being coached. First, the coach always starts off with the understanding that the person being coached has the capacity within them to solve the vast majority of their challenges. In a Christian context, I would add that the person being coached has the ability to hear from God and be the primary agent in clarifying their own agenda. Contrast this relationship to the process of mentoring, where an expert is the mentor and the client depends on the expert to tell them what to do.

Second, because the coach believes that an individual or team can hear from the Holy Spirit and think through their own challenges and opportunities, the coach's default mode is to ask questions rather than to give answers. The coach might occasionally offer suggestions, as will be discussed later in this chapter, but the coach first and foremost wants to help the person being coached to unpack their own thinking to the fullest.

Third, the coach helps the person being coached consider their situation from all facets. For example, a coach will likely begin by helping that individual develop a plan to address particular challenges or opportunities. The coach may then ask, "What could derail this plan?" or "What might be missing from this plan?" This allows the person being coached to look at their situation from different perspectives and modify their plan accordingly.

The coach also provides a level of accountability to the person they are coaching. The person being coached sets the purpose for the coaching relationship and only commits to action plans that they are comfortable with. Having a coaching relationship means that the coach will check in with the person during their next session. The person being coached will talk about progress and pitfalls since the last coaching session. This individual is not in trouble with the coach if they don't do what they have committed to doing, but having a meeting where goals are discussed helps ensure the person being coached is involved in an action plan.

WHY COACHING? WOULDN'T IT BE EASIER TO TELL PEOPLE WHAT TO DO?

Oftentimes, we want to approach discipleship relationships like traditional mentor-mentee relationships. We think that it is faster and more effective to tell people what to do than to accompany them through a careful, deliberative process. The example of Shari and Emily at the beginning of this chapter assumed that the discipleship relationship would involve someone who is older and more spiritually mature pouring into someone who is younger and less spiritually mature. There are certainly times for these types of relationships. However, in most discipling relationships, a coaching posture will be much more effective long term, for two very important reasons.

First, people tend to make greater progress on action plans that they create versus plans that are prescribed. I learned this early on in my ministry career. People would come to my office for counseling. I thought of myself as pretty insightful, so within a relatively short period of time, I would tell them what to do. If they followed my direction, I assured them, then things would turn out relatively well. I certainly recognized that some situations were especially challenging and couldn't be fixed with simple answers. But most of the time, I thought I could give people a list of three things they should start doing and three things they should stop doing and everything would be great.

In many cases, I might have even been correct about my prescription! The track record of people doing what I told them to do was relatively unimpressive, however. I think of numerous pastoral-counseling situations when people came into my office wanting advice about what to do in a situation. I would give them advice, and most of the time, they would incorporate only a small portion of the suggestion. They would return to my office asking my advice again, yet they hadn't done what I suggested previously.

I later switched my methodology to that of a coach. I helped the person articulate the situation and their ideas about handling the situation. Through the conversation, the solution would become apparent to them as they were processing. And then I noticed something: Individuals were much more likely to follow through on the action plans they had articulated than solutions I prescribed. I just needed to ask clarifying questions to help test and refine their plans.

I was in a group of coaches who were talking about this concept when one person said, "I have learned that a half-baked idea from the client is better than a full-baked idea from me." When we help people design the type of action plans that we discussed in the previous chapter, they are much more likely to follow through on that discipleship design than if we were to design an action plan for them and hand it to them to execute. A person's discipleship design may not be perfect, and it may not be exactly how we would have designed it, but the disciple will be able to grow much more effectively if we allow him or her to create that design.

The second reason that a coaching model is effective is that the person who helps the other person grow as a disciple doesn't need to be an expert or have significantly more knowledge than the person they are coaching. In fact, just as a sports coach may not be as good as the player she coaches, so may a person be less spiritually mature and still help someone else grow in their discipleship.

A coaching approach to making disciples allows for a greater opportunity for reproducing disciples. Both the model of discipleship presented in the previous chapter and the coaching approach to helping people in discipleship are relatively simple. A simple process is easily repeatable and reproducible, and since the person who is discipling others doesn't need to have all of the answers and isn't trying to clone themselves in the individual, it takes the pressure off. Shari doesn't have to worry about giving Emily the wrong advice about raising her children in the faith. She doesn't have to know everything there is to know about parenting or discipling children. She simply needs to rely on the Lord while she listens to Emily and asks questions to help Emily develop her own solutions.

HOW DO I COACH IN A DISCIPLESHIP RELATIONSHIP?

Hopefully the idea of using a coaching approach to disciple making makes sense and resonates with you. The next logical question, then, is, How might you go about that process of coaching someone to develop a plan for discipleship? The normal coaching process is fairly fluid and nonlinear; however, for the sake of simplicity, I will propose a linear process. As you continue to practice coaching people for discipleship, you are encouraged to adapt the process in a way that suits you.

STEP 1: Clarify the Goal of the Discipleship Design

It is helpful to guide someone toward clarity about where they want to be after the discipleship design is finished. This clarification process—going from a broad and undefined goal to one that is more precise and defined—usually takes several questions. Typically, I begin by asking a question like "Given the results of your simple discipleship assessment and other influences in your life, which area would you like to work on?" Sometimes a person doesn't have a very clear idea of the direction they want to go. In these cases, I ask further questions, such as "What did you learn from your assessment?" If the person hasn't completed an assessment, I might ask, "How would your spouse say you should grow in order to become more Christlike?" Another question I might ask is "Who do you admire as a Christian—and why?" These types of questions can help stimulate thinking about a person's current spiritual maturity and where God might be calling them in the future.

Sometimes, when I first ask about an area where someone might want to grow, the individual has some good initial thoughts. For example, someone might say, "I want to be more loving," "I want to have a better understanding of theology," or "I want to find out what God wants me to do." These are fantastic starts to get an idea of where someone wants to grow. These answers need to further crystallize, however, in order to be most effective. Therefore, I might ask, "Why is being more loving something you want to work on?" The answer to this might narrow down the focus. Perhaps the person wants to be more loving to the people they work with, or perhaps they want to be more loving to their family. Perhaps when they answer this question, what they really mean by "more loving" is that they want to be more patient, which is a different characteristic in the discipleship profile. It is important that the person paint a picture of what they want to be true about their life after completing the plan. This picture needs to be in their own words and will motivate them to follow through on the plan.

We also want to ensure that the goals people set for themselves have a particular time element and some form of measurement associated with them. Some examples of clear statements include

- "By June of next year, I want to be able to name all of the books of the New Testament and identify the author, audience, and primary purpose of each one."
- "By January, I will have identified my spiritual gifts and committed to serving in a way that utilizes those gifts."

- "By April, I want to be more comfortable sharing my faith with others and will have done so with five people who are not yet believers."
- "By October, my kids will experience me as more patient and attentive to their needs."

Notice that some of the statements have very clear metrics, such as sharing one's faith with five people. Other statements have softer metrics, such as someone's kids experiencing their parent as more patient and attentive. If someone develops an outcome with a softer type of metric, then you might ask how that person will be able to celebrate progress.

If someone develops a goal that is not time constrained or their plan lacks specificity, then you will want to ask questions to help them develop these elements. Examples of some questions to clarify focus can be things like

- "What will it look like when you are finished with your design?"
- "How will you know if you have grown in the area you are focusing on?"

STEP 2: Clarify Activities

Once a goal is determined, it is important to clarify the activities that will help achieve that goal. It is helpful to have activities that connect to each of the four directions (see the previous chapter). For some disciples, I sit down with a piece of paper or a whiteboard and create four boxes for the different activity types. I then ask the disciple to fill in the various activities.

Date:

Name:

Topic of Focus:

Goal:

ACTIVITIES TO ENGAGE WITH GOD (Spiritual)	ACTIVITIES TO ENGAGE WITH EXPERIENCE (Experiential)
ACTIVITIES TO ENGAGE WITH OTHERS (Relational)	ACTIVITIES TO ENGAGE WITH KNOWLEDGE AND TRUTH (Instructional)

Some people will be able to do those things relatively easily; others will want to brainstorm a lot of possibilities and then narrow the list down to the ones they actually want to commit to. For other people, I ask a question related to each category, such as "How can you engage with God in order to grow in the way you have articulated in your previously specified goal?"

When people develop particular action plans, we want to ensure that these plans are also concrete and time specific. For example, an action needs to be more than simply "I will read my Bible more." We don't want to be legalistic or think of these things as simply boxes to check, but we want to make sure each element has clarity behind it. A better action plan is "Each day, I will read a chapter from the Gospel of John and journal about what I read." If I am working with someone who says they want to read their Bible more, I ask some follow-up questions, such as *How often? Which parts of the Bible?* and *Besides reading passages, what else are you going to do?*

A similar process occurs when developing action plans associated with other areas of growth. If someone desires to be more present and patient with their kids, I might ask, "What times do you notice your lack of presence?" They might indicate that they tend to be distracted at dinner and think people should be present with their families during mealtimes. I might ask what things cause distractions. The answer might be looking at their cell phone during meals. I might then ask, "What can be done about this challenge?" The person might say that nothing can be done because they have to have the phone with them for emergencies. On the other hand, they might indicate that they can put the phone aside during dinner and only return to it an hour afterward.

STEP 3: Find the Holes in the Plan

Once someone has filled activities in all four boxes, it is time to test the sufficiency of that person's plan. Usually, I ask questions that help people uncover potential flaws. I might say, "Compare your overall goal with your plan. What is missing in your plan?" This helps the person think through whether their plan for discipleship will actually produce the desired goal. Along this line, I might also work from each action step toward the desired outcome: If they fulfill this particular action step, what will be produced as a result? Is it in line with their overall goal?

I might also ask where they are tempted to not follow

through with their plan. A person might indicate that while they have every intention of having time in the morning with God, they have tried it before and often don't fulfill that desire. At this point, I ask what they need to put in place to ensure they follow through with their plan. They may indicate that they won't eat breakfast, including having coffee, until they have had a quiet time. They might say that they won't check e-mails until they have their quiet time, because e-mails often lead them down a rabbit trail away from the Scriptures. Others' responsibilities make a regular and consistent time for morning devotions impossible; therefore, another approach might be developed.

I also often ask what a person will need to *stop doing* in order to fulfill their action plan. Many of us are so busy that we try to cram our relationship with God into the cracks of the various things going on in our lives. When we take this approach, we often have minimal success in our action plan. If we are willing to stop doing certain things in order to make time for our discipleship design, however, our chance of fulfilling our design increases. A person might therefore say that they are going to not watch TV at night in order to go to bed earlier so they can wake up earlier and have time with the Lord. A person might say that they are going to spend less time socializing in order to fulfill their discipleship design or replace their previous reading of celebrity biographies with reading Scripture or theological or devotional books.

Sometimes when you are working with a person and developing an action plan, you wonder if you can ever give advice. Do you always have to ask questions? There are times when it is appropriate to give advice; however, it is wise to use a few guidelines in doing so. First, make sure a person has unpacked their own thinking fully. Ask questions, from different angles if need be, in order to help someone process their own situations and needs. It is very easy to jump in too quickly with your own solution and not allow the person to fully process their position.

Second, we want to make sure that if we *do* give advice, the person is free to take or leave the advice that we give. For example, someone might indicate that they have no time to engage in their discipleship design. You may ask multiple times what that individual can cut in order to fulfill their plan, and they may not have any ideas. You may then ask if you can give a suggestion, such as going to bed earlier in order to wake up earlier and therefore have more time in the morning. This might be a great idea, but the person may be hesitant to do so for whatever reason. When you help a person develop a design, they need to be free to disregard potential actions that you might recommend. I have seen people pressured into putting things on their discipleship designs that they don't really want to work toward. The majority of the time that this happens, people end up not doing what they put on their designs in the first place because they didn't own it for themselves.

A FEW NOTES ABOUT POWERFUL QUESTIONS

Without going too deep into coaching methodology, here are a few helpful suggestions for asking powerful questions:

- Ask open-ended questions: Powerful questions can't be answered with a simple *yes* or *no*. Questions should therefore start with words like *how, what, where, when,* and the like. Close-ended questions, such as those that start with *is, are, will, can,* and the like, are usually not powerful questions.

- Ask one question at a time: Sometimes we are tempted to ask two questions simultaneously. We might ask, for example, "What things are you going to do, and when are you going to do them?" People need time to think through one question fully before they tackle a second one.

- Silence is golden: Do you know when you have asked a good question? It is when the person pauses to think through their answer. Do you know what you do when there is silence? You stay silent. You don't need to repeat or reword the question. The person is thinking and needs that space to think uninterrupted. If they need more information or want you to rephrase the question, they will ask you to do so.

Most of us have a default position: We are accustomed to one person telling another person what to do. This can especially be true during times where one person has more experience or expertise. There's certainly nothing wrong with mentoring relationships, but we simplify discipleship—for both the disciple and the person discipling them—if we shift our approach from mentoring to coaching. We will see greater benefits in individual discipleship and increase the capacity for multiplying disciples in the process.

REFLECTION QUESTIONS

1. Can you think of a time when you have processed a problem out loud with someone and come to a good conclusion without the other person giving advice? Maybe you have been that person helping another to process their situation. What was that like?

2. How would you describe the difference between a mentor and a coach? In what situations are mentors helpful, and in what situations are coaches helpful?

3. How does it relieve pressure in discipling another person to think of yourself as a coach?

4. What excites you about coaching another person in discipleship? What makes you nervous?

5. What remaining questions do you have about coaching?

CHAPTER 10

Strategies and Environments for Discipleship

SUSAN WAS EXCITED TO have a renewed emphasis on discipleship in the church she was pastoring. She had talked for months with the elders about the nature of discipleship. They had spent a lot of time assessing the spiritual health of the church members. They also took a hard look at the effectiveness of their current ministry efforts in developing disciples. These assessments were eye-opening—they knew significant changes needed to be made to their disciple-making system. The question was, How should the church go about these changes? How could the church infuse its culture with discipleship where it hadn't existed previously?

One elder chimed in. "Our older members love the Sunday-school classes that they have been attending for thirty to forty years. I want to make sure we don't send a message to them that could negate their positive experiences." Another said, "We just did a push to change a small-group model. We need to be careful of another major change." Others were concerned about what to do with the programs that had more of a social aspect but were not particularly focused on making disciples.

While the elders were now excited about focusing on making disciples, they knew that implementing deeper aspects of discipleship development in their church was going to be challenging. They needed to spend some time developing a strategy in order to increase the chance of success.

Implementing any kind of change is challenging. The conversation at Susan's church illustrates the challenges churches face as they seek to have a greater focus on discipleship. There are phenomenal books written on negotiating change individually and organizationally. This chapter will first focus on some high-level and basic principles that churches and their leadership can use. The second part will focus on different environments within a church where the simple discipleship concepts can be easily incorporated.

The purpose of this chapter is to help the leaders of a church take the information from the previous two chapters and find an appropriate way to implement it in the life of their congregation. The hope is that these leaders will find a way to introduce the concept of having individuals evaluate their own discipleship and create a design for their personal discipleship. Leaders can use the principles of change in this chapter as well as suggestions for introducing discipleship in different environments to create a strategy for growth.

IMPLEMENTING CHANGE

One of the best book titles I have seen is *How to Change Your Church without Killing It* by Alan Nelson and Gene Appel.[1] This is the challenge that churches face when bringing about change. Change is needed so churches don't die, but at the same time, the process of bringing about those necessary changes can be done poorly and essentially kill the church. Below are some high-level change strategies that are especially pertinent to the process of transforming a church culture toward discipleship.

Run Experiments with Motivated Participants

Sometimes churches will seek to force a change on everyone, which can be met with significant resistance. Some changes that a church must make will necessarily impact the whole congregation, such as changing worship schedules, moving locations, or building a new sanctuary. Changing a culture toward discipleship, however, can be done without immediately influencing the entire congregation. In fact, a few motivated individuals can engage in some pilot and experimental groups that are separate from what the whole congregation is doing but that can set the table for wider change.

One of the environments for discipleship that will be presented below is having groups of two or three people, ordinarily of the same gender, where no real leader is needed. In one church I served, there was a focus on small groups that picked their own curriculum. I had three women who wanted to join a small group; however, they could not find a time and place that worked for their schedules. This was at the same time when I wanted to change the culture to be more discipleship focused. I met with these three women and proposed that they experiment with being a discipleship triad. I told them that they didn't need a designated leader for this group, and that I was happy to answer questions or give suggestions as their group met. These women found the experience to be fantastic and also offered some suggestions about how to help other discipleship groups in early stages of development.

This approach was very helpful in that we could start this group without making any changes to the overall structure of the ministry. We also learned from this experiment before getting a lot of other members of the congregation involved. An additional benefit of starting with the pilot group was that these ladies championed this approach going forward. Having someone other than the pastor or a paid ministry leader promoting a ministry is invaluable to achieving overall success.

As you look for people to try something new, you may want to keep in mind that sometimes your existing leaders are not the ideal ones to begin pilot projects. Oftentimes, those who are doing well—or think they are doing well—in existing ministries are least likely to want to do something different because they don't have a sense of urgency. Look instead for those who may be disenfranchised with existing ministries or haven't found a way to connect through the church's discipleship ministry. These individuals will be more likely and willing to try something new because what already exists doesn't work for them.

Celebrate What You Want to Replicate

I love the phrase "Celebrate what you want to replicate." It makes sense that the stories you tell and the things you celebrate with the congregation are the things that are most likely to continue to take place in the future. As you begin pilot projects in any number of discipleship environments, take the opportunity to lift the successes. Use sermon illustrations from these groups. Have those that have experienced life change share their stories with the church.

Sharing success stories with the congregation does a couple of things. First, it helps to spark the heart of those who may be feeling stuck in their own discipleship. They may choose to participate in one of the discipleship opportunities that will be offered or created later. We even had some people hear the testimonies of others and start their own triad groups without telling the church's leaders.

Second, sharing these stories of success indicates what is valuable to the church's ministry. I have seen churches with an evangelism candle. Whenever someone comes to faith, they light the candle and share the story. These stories tell other people in the church that evangelism is celebrated by the church and is the responsibility of not just the ministries of the church but also its members.

Marry Discipleship with Other Ministries

I had a coach who told me, "The best way to change DNA is not through small changes but rather through reproduction." Because I had a background of studying biology, this coach knew I would get the analogy: The best way to change the DNA of a church is to comingle the new ministry with something that already exists. This strategy makes sense and it works—especially with ministries that are already open to revitalization. A ministry that is already working well can serve as a host to get the new vision into the culture's DNA.

For example, Susan could go to the Sunday-school class of forty years and work with them to bring this new emphasis on discipleship into their class. This would certainly be preferable to telling the Sunday school that their ministry is no longer viable and they need to abandon it to do something completely different. I faced a situation like that at a church I served. The church had heard good things about church-wide campaigns—such as 40 Days of Purpose—to help build a small-group ministry. Unfortunately, the way this got communicated was by suggesting that Sunday school was bad and small groups were good. Two long-term Sunday-school classes were told to disband and reform as midweek small groups. Most of the people in those Sunday school classes didn't drive at night! And they resented the insinuation that their approach was bad. A better way to have handled the situation would have been to identify unique ways the Sunday school could join in the church-wide campaign for that brief season while continuing to gather on Sunday mornings. This way, class members would have felt valued and encouraged.

There are other ways to merge a DNA of discipleship with something that is already occurring. One church had monthly small-group leadership meetings. These meetings were getting a little stale, as they were to train people and yet with the diversity of skills among the leaders, they couldn't train everyone at the same time. Instead, they had each of the small-group leaders develop a personal design for discipleship and teach it to the other small-group leaders. This process was remarkably successful. It ended up incorporating several of the principles mentioned so far.

ENVIRONMENTS FOR DISCIPLESHIP

The advantage of simple discipleship is that it can be incorporated into a range of different environments. A church can intentionally bring these principles and resources into a variety of situations, depending on the various needs of the congregation. Below are three types of groups that can either incorporate this model of discipleship or be established by using this model of discipleship. I will present each model and provide options for the variety of ways the group can utilize the simple discipleship assessment process to create and implement personalized discipleship designs.

One-on-One Discipleship Relationships

Normally, when we think about one-on-one relationships, we think of mentoring—someone who is more mature in the faith imparting wisdom and knowledge to someone who is less mature in the faith, perhaps even a brand-new believer. This is certainly one valuable way that one-on-one discipleship can occur; however, peer-to-peer relationships can also be extremely effective, especially when the principles and resources of simple discipleship are employed.

When a one-on-one mentoring relationship is formed, ordinarily it would only be the less mature person who takes an assessment and develops a design for discipleship around their results. (Of course, the more mature person should also attend to their personal discipleship, but that is not the function of this particular relationship.)

The design for a person's discipleship can be obtained a number of ways. The disciple might take the simple discipleship assessment. If a disciple is a brand-new believer, however, the assessment might be a little overwhelming and perhaps even a little discouraging because they will likely score low in all areas. In that case, I recommend that the more mature disciple help the newer disciple arrive at a design for discipleship through a series of questions to the individual. As the person grows in the faith, they'll reach a point where the simple discipleship assessment will be more useful to them.

I recently worked with a brand-new disciple who was a stay-at-home dad. His wife had been a believer for years and was thrilled that her husband had come to faith in Jesus. If I had given the man an assessment of discipleship at that point, however, it would have pointed out so many areas that needed to be developed that he would have been deeply discouraged. This guy didn't even know there were two Testaments in Scripture; he didn't even know the word *Trinity*! He also didn't have relationships with Christians who could assess his discipleship, as his wife was the only Christian with whom he had any depth of relationship. Therefore, I asked him a series of questions to help him discover where he wanted to start growing. I had some ideas, but rather than me telling him where he should start to focus, I wanted him to own his discipleship.

We talked awhile and came up with two things he wanted to be able to do. First, he wanted to learn how to pray. His conversion experience occurred as he was by himself and reflecting on the passing of his mother two years earlier. He contacted the pastor who had performed his wedding and began to share some of what he was feeling. The pastor helped him to see that this experience was God nudging his heart. The man was intrigued that he could talk to God and wanted to develop that practice. We therefore developed a design to grow in this area of discipleship.

In his design, the stay-at-home dad engaged with God (the first direction) by practicing different types of prayer exercises. One week, he did the ACTS prayer (starting with adoration, then confession, then thanksgiving, and finally, supplication). Another week, he did some reflective reading from the Psalms in a modified *lectio divina* approach,[2] and then another week he did an examen type of prayer twice a day. Each week, we would talk about his experience. He engaged with truth (the second direction) in that he was reading from the Gospels with the lens of viewing what Jesus did and taught related to prayer. This allowed him to not only work on his desire to grow in prayer but also get into the Scriptures in a way that linked to where he was already motivated to grow. He engaged with community (the third direction) in that he was talking about his prayer life with me and his wife. And finally, he was engaged experientially (the fourth direction) by not only leaning into the Christian life he had entered but also praying regularly with his wife and with me.

My relationship with this man certainly had some aspects of a typical mentor-mentee format: I made some suggestions and gave him resources he wouldn't normally have had access to. I allowed him to be much more involved in the development of his own discipleship design than would be the case in a typical mentoring relationship, however. This process took longer than me simply telling him what to do, but in the end, he was much more committed to his action plan. The added benefit was that he wasn't as reliant on me for his growth in discipleship but was learning to listen to God and think through his own action plans.

Triad/Leaderless Relationships

Another helpful format to help facilitate discipleship is a very small group of people that has no identified leader. The typical number for such a group is three people (which is why it's often referred to as a triad); however, leaderless relationships can be done effectively with four people or in a one-on-one relationship. When this group is made up of two people, it is distinguished from the one-on-one relationship mentioned above in that the discipling relationship is mutual, with each person helping the other toward growth and development.

A triad or leaderless group can be effective in that no one feels the pressure to live up to the qualifications of a leader. A leaderless group also helps solidify the understanding that each person has the capacity to hear from God directly—no one is reliant upon an expert. It is also easier for these groups to multiply, since the health of the group doesn't depend on the talent of a particular leader.

A leaderless group does, nevertheless, need to establish the dynamics that are going to be present for the group. Establishing these dynamics includes creating the rules by which the group will function. These agreements can include things like understanding that whatever is said in the group is completely confidential, or that group members only give advice to each other when asked to do so. The agreements (or "covenants") that these individuals make to each other will change from group to group and should be reviewed periodically to determine whether any changes are needed. Because of the nature of what is discussed in these groups, it is often advantageous to keep them gender specific, especially with one-on-one relationships.

This group should also determine a format for their time together. Some groups will have longer meetings three to four times a year, so that they can develop their own plan for discipleship. In these meetings, group members might spend an hour or two focusing on each person, praying and helping that person process the nature of their discipleship design, and then switch to another individual.

Instead of doing one longer session, some groups take three to four weeks and focus one week on each person as they develop their design. Once each member has created their design, group members continue to get together each week to talk about implementing their designs. They ask each other where their designs are going well and producing the desired outcome and inquire about places where they might be getting stuck and having a difficult time living out their designs.

Some groups spend half an hour on each individual. For the first ten minutes, one group member talks about how God has been working in their life and then for ten to fifteen minutes, the others ask the person probing questions to continue to stimulate their growth. Then, in the last five minutes, they pray for that disciple and shift their attention to the next person. Some groups have a shared Scripture that they are reading and reflecting on; in this case, the group might spend an hour going over the Scriptures together and then thirty minutes (ten minutes for each person) reflecting on how God is working through their designs.

These triads are a built-in format for people to live out the part of their design that involves community (the third direction). This triad community prays not only for each member of the group to fulfill their design but also that God would work in their lives to produce the desired fruit. This community keeps each other accountable to fulfill their designs and provides an opportunity for each disciple to process how God is working in their midst.

Small-Group Format

Another way to live out the development of a discipleship design based upon the results of the simple discipleship assessment is to do it in an established small-group format. This is probably the least effective of the three environments to create and live out one's discipleship design (because established small groups have an existing culture). However, given the principle above about introducing DNA into an existing structure, this might be a good starting point for a small group. It is unlikely that a small group that is already thriving will want to dramatically alter to introduce this type of discipleship, but incremental steps can be made.

One way to do so is to have an existing small group be introduced to the concept of the simple discipleship assessment. The group can study and reflect upon the qualities and characteristics. If the group wishes, they can all take the simple discipleship assessment during the week. (Bulk assessments can be purchased at a discount at the website www.flourish movement.org.) Or, instead of taking the assessment, small-group members might review the qualities and characteristics and pick a particular area where they would like to grow.

The next time the group meets, the basic four activities that need to be present in a discipleship design could be introduced. The group can take half an hour to help one person develop a design for their life. The group can then break off into pairs or triads to help each other develop a personal discipleship design. Then, as the group continues to meet weekly, they can incorporate a check-in regarding their individual designs for discipleship. This allows the small group to continue to engage in whatever study they would normally participate in. A small group may, for example, ordinarily study and reflect on the passage from the previous or upcoming sermon. The group can continue to spend most of their time in the small group engaging in this type of study and still have some time to check in with one another regarding the progress of their individual discipleship designs.

There are a variety of ways in which a church can implement the simple discipleship concepts into the existing ministry structure or use the concepts to create new mechanisms for discipleship. Some churches will choose to try the concepts with a pilot small group or just among the leaders of the volunteer ministries. Some churches allow the existing structure to stay in place and encourage simple discipleship in new types of relationships. The key for churches is to ask how the concepts will best be implemented within the church.

The intention in this book is to simplify discipleship as a way to prioritize it. Discipleship happens best when each person approaches their own discipleship in a way that is personalized to how God is already at work in their life. I find that the Lord is gracious to me and helps me to know that while my discipleship will never be perfect on this side of heaven, He faithfully helps me focus on one area at a time. As the Lord helps me grow in that area, I find that not only does He produce newness in my life but also that the journey He allows me to experience is just as rewarding as the destination.

My hope is that as you simplify discipleship in your life, in your personal relationships, and in your church, you will find an increasing level of joy and satisfaction in your life and in the lives of those around you.

REFLECTION QUESTIONS

1. What were your most significant learnings from this book?

2. Who in your congregation or among your relationships do you think might be attracted to this model of discipleship?

3. Who in your congregation or among your relationships might get excited about engaging in this model of discipleship with you?

4. Where might you start implementing the concepts of simple discipleship? Would it be best in your context to start with a pilot group, new members, a group of leaders, or another format?

5. What can you do to help bring about discipleship transformation in your life, in the lives of others, and in your congregation?

Conclusion

The greatest issue facing the world today, with all its heartbreaking needs, is whether those who, by profession or culture, are identified as "Christians" will become disciples—students, apprentices, practitioners—of Jesus Christ, steadily learning from him how to live the life of the Kingdom of the Heavens into every corner of human existence.

DALLAS WILLARD, *The Great Omission: Reclaiming Jesus's Essential Teachings on Discipleship*

THIS QUOTE FROM DALLAS WILLARD has always caused me to reflect on the function of my ministry. I can get sidetracked by budgetary concerns, staffing challenges, or strategic planning—things that may only marginally relate to making disciples. I know that I am not alone in this frustration: I talk to numerous pastors and lay leaders who realize that much of the activity at their churches is not about making or maturing disciples. At best, these activities only scratch the surface of discipleship; at worst, they simply provide opportunities to entertain and socialize.

We surveyed pastors and lay leaders in our denomination, asking where they needed the greatest help from the denomination. Survey participants had to rank their needs from greatest to least. The number one challenge of our pastors—the place where they indicated the greatest need—was in making disciples. Their desire was on both ends of the spectrum: to help their current members mature in faith and to strive to reach more people for Jesus.

I do not think it is an exaggeration to say that we are facing a discipleship crisis. The one advantage that we have now as compared to a few decades ago is that we are recognizing and naming the challenge. We are no longer content with setting the bar of Christian faith at attending church, with little-to-no impact on daily lives.

It is ironic that in Western cultures, the places with the greatest wealth and education, we are arguably the least effective in making and maturing disciples. We look at the explosion of the gospel historically in Africa, Asia, and South America, which have seen the viral spread of the Good News. More recently, we see the gospel penetrate the Middle East in ways that are almost unimaginable.

WHAT WE LEARN FROM THE GLOBAL CHURCH

As I was writing this book, I had the occasion to interact with several ministry leaders from countries where the gospel is having a major impact. I have sat with house-church leaders from these very hostile and closed countries. I have heard incredible stories of God's work. Not only were new people coming to faith in Jesus, but also the depth of discipleship in the leaders and members was palpable.

I sat with one man in his late twenties who leads a small house-church fellowship of around twenty people. He has no formal biblical education or ministry training. He lost his job and his home and has been imprisoned multiple times because of his work for God's Kingdom. As I interacted with him, I experienced the depth of his faith and dedication to Jesus. He fulfills what Dallas Willard identified as our culture's greatest need: not a Christian in name only, but a true disciple of Jesus Christ, one who strives to bring the Kingdom of Heaven to earth.

Because of this book, I began to ask different questions of these leaders than I had with similar leaders in the past. I asked about the process by which they mature disciples and train leaders. I knew they most likely did not have a lot of training material, financial resources, or opportunity to gather large groups of people together. I knew they needed a relatively simple process that could be easily replicated in a variety of situations. I was pleasantly surprised to discover that the vast majority employ similar principles to those that have been described in this book, contextualized for their particular situations.

The first thing that all of these leaders did was to identify where a person needed to grow at that particular time. This is the point of the simple discipleship assessment discussed in this book: a starting point to help people—in conversation with others—identify where God is calling them to grow.

The leaders in this global church did not have a formalized assessment. In their contexts, they can have conversations naturally that the assessment is meant to foster. Disciples at all points in their walk with Christ have people who are investing in their lives, helping them to grow more in the likeness of Christ. On some occasions, a disciple is a newer believer and has someone more spiritually mature that helps them grow. These more mature believers have a natural understanding of a disciple and a grid, even if informal, that they use to help newer disciples understand places that they should grow in the likeness of Christ.

More mature believers usually have groups of people around them who are also mature. These groups function in a spirit of mutual encouragement—they are committed to praying for and encouraging each other, and holding one another accountable for growing in faith.

From underground house churches to churches that have tens of thousands of people, the primary place of discipleship is in individual or small-group relationships, and the primary driver of the process is the question of where this person needs to grow.

The second similarity I've observed in growing churches all over the world is *how* people tend to develop disciples once a place of need has been identified. I interacted with some leaders who use a method very similar to what's detailed in chapter 8, but many others simply intuit how to help another person grow in their relationship with Jesus. Even in this intuitive process, the basic elements laid out in chapter 8 are present. Leaders may not use the language of "engage with God, engage with others, engage with experience, and engage with knowledge and truth," but they weave these things together as they help others grow.

Everyone helped their disciples find a way to enhance their prayer lives or utilize their spiritual disciplines. Everyone helped them examine their hearts within the day or week. I saw traces of ways in which disciples were encouraged to study Scripture and/or other material (as they had access, which was quite limited in some countries) pertinent to where God was calling them to grow. I saw how leaders could form disciples in community and ways in which disciples were encouraged to have prayer partners or other people in their lives that could help them grow. I also saw in every case that disciples were given practical experiences where they would be tested and grow in skill, character, and knowledge. I asked leaders about incorporating these elements, and all of them indicated that unless people know that they will have to apply what they are learning, they won't learn and grow.

The one thing that varied significantly in different contexts was the way in which the mentor or disciple maker interacted with the person they were helping grow as a disciple. Most of the time, the person who was helping another grow was fairly directive. The discipleship relationships tended to be hierarchical; it was a rare occasion even for more mature believers to have opportunities for mutual encouragement. I gather from conversations that there are significant cultural reasons why a hierarchical form of ministry works well and people can follow through on assignments given by those in power; however, I do think that in Western culture, a more self-directed coaching model works well. Discipling relationships with newer believers will need to be more instructive, of course, as newer disciples will not know what they don't know and therefore will not naturally be able to find solutions to their discipleship challenges. Even in these beginning stages of relationships, however, if you can find the opportunity to help the disciples think for themselves, it will help them greatly in the long run, equipping them to easily disciple others.

I hope it is encouraging to see that where the gospel is growing, people are using the concepts of *Simple Discipleship*.

I wonder whether when Jesus sends out the seventy-two disciples in Luke 10, part of the reason He tells them not to bring extra supplies, money, and tools is not only that they would depend on the tools rather than the Lord but also that having so many tools would make it harder for future generations to replicate their ministries. When people engage in simple discipleship—as leaders must do in other parts of the world—it makes the art of making disciples much more reproducible.

 ## TAKING THE NEXT STEPS WITH YOUR CHURCH

For those reading this book who are church pastors, church staff, or lay leaders, and are responsible for the overall culture and strategy of discipleship, the thought of implementing the strategies associated with simple discipleship may seem daunting. Oftentimes, our discipleship programs have grown haphazardly, so moving into a simple discipleship model will eventually mean cutting or changing ministries that don't produce fruit. These potential changes could stop you in your tracks, reminding you of the challenge and pushback you will face. Below are a few suggested ways to begin incorporating the process of simple discipleship into your church. You may want to use one of these options, or they may inspire you to think of other strategies that will work well in your context.

Start Small

Find a couple of new disciples who are hungry and ready to grow. This option can work well if you are the pastor of a smaller church or you are a staff member or lay leader. This doesn't require you to change any existing program or ministry. The newer disciples can still engage in other small-group or discipleship ministries within your church, but this can be a way of specifically helping a new disciple grow in their faith. You may not want to use the assessment with these new believers, as the results can be an overwhelming reminder of how much room they have for growth as Christians. You can ask the disciples where they would like to grow in their relationship with the Lord, their knowledge of Him and His Word, or how they can be used by Him.

One of the first times I used the design process outlined in this book was with a brand-new disciple. He was hungry to grow in faith and came to me with a lot of questions about the nature of Jesus and how to know your purpose in life. I told him that while I could give him a lot of information, he would learn more deeply and better apply his knowledge if I helped him discover the answers for himself. I asked him if he wanted to focus a couple of months on answering these questions at a deeper and more personal level. He was excited to truly explore these subjects rather than having me give him the Sunday-school answers.

I helped him create a design around these topics, and because he was a new disciple, I suggested some resources that would be helpful, considering his background. I then helped him create a plan that involved others and gave him some practical experiences to use his newfound knowledge. Part of his homework was to teach some of the basic concepts about Jesus to his seven-year-old son. Not only did this motivate him to do the reading and reflection with me, but also it helped him internalize and crystallize his newfound knowledge. We went on to create other discipleship plans, and he became a big proponent of the process. He has also helped other people create similar discipleship plans.

Put a Team Together

Another option is doing discipleship designs with a group of leaders, such as elders or small-group leaders. It would be easy for a leadership team to take the discipleship assessment and process the results with others who are close to them. They could determine an area to grow, and then, during an elder or leader meeting, they could help one another create discipleship plans and share them with the whole group (or a portion of the group).

There are multiple advantages to this approach. First, it helps ensure that your elders and leaders are examining their own spiritual life and areas of growth. Unfortunately, elders that focus on these things seem to be more the exception than the norm. Changing the dynamics of these meetings and spending some time creating discipleship plans, sharing those plans, and checking in with these plans will increase the spiritual depth of your leaders and your conversations.

The second advantage to this approach is that your leaders will see some significant growth in their own lives and be convinced of the principles of simple discipleship. They will then be more likely to incorporate these principles in other ministries in which they are involved. If they are small-group leaders, then they can continue to lead their small groups in similar formats, but perhaps take a couple of weeks to talk about the profile of a disciple and help their group members determine areas of growth and create designs accordingly. Then, during normal small-group time in subsequent weeks, they can check in or pray about the design process.

Church-Wide Campaign

A final option presented here (although there are probably numerous more elsewhere) is to create a church-wide focus on discipleship. Perhaps have a preaching or teaching series around the qualities and characteristics of a disciple. You might then offer a class in developing discipleship designs or train a few people to help others create discipleship designs. While on the surface this is more of a public launch than a private one, many churches are used to having small-group questions built around sermon series, so this provides an opportunity for broader exposure in a rhythm that might be familiar. If you do take this approach, I encourage trying some things out with a smaller group first to experience some preliminary wins before engaging in a church-wide process.

FINAL ENCOURAGEMENT

Periodically, I take time to examine my ministry calling and history. I think about when I was a junior in high school and co-led a weekend event for high-school students. I think of being a volunteer leader and then a paid leader for a student ministry when I was in college. I think of the first message I gave in "big church" (on abiding in Christ). I think of my call to seminary, to my first church as solo pastor, and later to my first church as a senior pastor, and finally to my present position as the executive of the denomination. I like to recall all of those calls because whether I could articulate it at the time or not, they all had one thing in common. Each one was birthed out of what have become the theme verses for my life.

> *Him we proclaim, warning everyone and teaching*
> *everyone with all wisdom, that we may present everyone*
> *mature in Christ. For this I toil, struggling with all his*
> *energy that he powerfully works within me.*
> COLOSSIANS 1:28-29

These verses have helped me reflect regularly on the nature and purpose of my call. I ask myself if my focus is truly to present everyone mature in Christ, or if I have been spinning my wheels in tangential activity. These verses call me back to realign my own efforts, focusing on developing a greater quantity of mature disciples. Then, like Paul, I want to work hard, I want to struggle with all of the effort and strength that God gives me toward that end.

I want to encourage you—whether you are a small-group leader, a staff member, a pastor, or anyone who wants to fulfill the mission of God to make disciples of all nations—to use this book and these verses to realign your focus toward presenting everyone mature in Christ. It will be challenging, it will be costly, and it will be tiring at times. It will, however, be *the* most rewarding experience ever as you see the fruit of the labor that you were designed in Christ to produce.

Acknowledgments

In the process of writing this book, I have had the opportunity to reflect on my own discipleship journey and the many people and churches that God has used to shape my soul, my understanding of discipleship, and, by extension, this book.

The most influential people in my life have been my family members—specifically, my parents. From an early age, I witnessed a desire to grow in maturity in Christ and apply scriptural truths to my life from my parents. They have always encouraged me to be who God has called me to be and extended unconditional love and grace throughout my growth process.

I am grateful for—and undeserving of—my wife, Beth. Her depth of faith and commitment to the Lord encourage and inspire me. She models the love of Jesus by showing grace and truth to those whom God has placed in her life, including me. She is naturally far better at helping others grow in maturity in faith than I am. Our children—Micah, Peyton, and Piper—are the greatest gifts God could have entrusted to us. They remind me that God has created each of us with different gifts and strengths to fulfill the unique calling that He has put on each of our lives.

The Lord has placed amazing people in my life who have pastored and encouraged me. These have been relationships of mutual encouragement, but my soul has been strengthened through our connection. David Hancock is one that I have had the privilege of raising into ministry, yet he has often served as my pastor. David has taught me more about what it means to embrace a gospel-saturated life than anyone else. He has helped me continually root my identity in Jesus when I am tempted to define myself by failures or successes.

I am indebted to churches that have taken chances on me and entrusted me with leadership responsibilities from an early age. I am grateful to have been raised in Goleta Presbyterian Church in Goleta, California. They hired me to be their youth director and gave me the opportunity to preach even when I was in college. Christ Presbyterian Church in Lakewood, California, called me as their pastor when I was twenty-five years old, after their previous two pastors had both retired in their positions. They taught and molded me more than I did them. Indian River Presbyterian Church in Fort Pierce, Florida, also provided me with great examples of faithful followers of Christ, loved my family and me well, and exemplified whole-life discipleship.

I am thankful to ECO: A Covenant Order of Evangelical Presbyterians and those who led the movement at the very beginning in order to shape a denomination that focuses on flourishing local churches that make disciples of Jesus Christ. Specifically, Jim Singleton, John Crosby, and John Ortberg have been deep influences in both ECO and my life. The three of you set a high bar! All of the staff that work with ECO are deeply committed to discipleship and living for Christ, and I am indebted to them—especially Lisa Johnson, John Terech, and Nate Dreesmann, with whom I collaborate most frequently on discipleship efforts. I am grateful for the pastors, elders, and churches across the country and throughout the world that are part of ECO. Your commitment to the gospel and enthusiastic participation in the mission of Jesus to see a great quantity and quality of disciples produced through your faithfulness is an inspiration and a blessing to me.

A Simple Discipleship Assessment

A KEY COMPONENT TO the premise of this book is that discipleship is personalized. The Lord's work for growth in a person's life at any given time is going to be different from the work He wants to do in another person's life. Therefore, while there are advantages to prepackaged group discipleship materials, the most effective way to grow as disciples is to focus deeply in an area where God is already cultivating work in our lives.

The challenge, however, can be to determine the place where God is seeking to bear fruit in our lives. I set out to design an assessment that could help an individual gauge their health as a disciple using both a self-evaluation and the input from others who know the disciple well. Creating an assessment to determine where God is at work initially seemed presumptuous and arrogant. However, tools such as spiritual-gift assessments have been very helpful for individuals seeking to understand themselves—so long as we understand that the tool does not replace leaning on the Spirit but can enhance our ability to see how God is working in our lives.

I worked with Dr. Gregory Wiens, who has a PhD in psychometrics and has guided the creation and validation process of numerous assessments. Dr. Wiens walked with me in the multi-step process to determine the simple discipleship assessment.

The first step was to articulate a picture of a disciple with qualities and characteristics synthesized from Scripture. These qualities and characteristics are described in chapters 4 through 7. The
process to determine these qualities was refined with the assis-
tance of a few dozen writers and practitioners who specialize in
discipleship. These individuals were helpful not only in crafting
the language to describe the qualities but also in participating in a
variety of assessments to confirm the validity of the qualities and
characteristics, ensuring that real-life examples could be easily
tied to established qualities and characteristics.

LIST OF QUALITIES AND CHARACTERISTICS

Quality #1 Gospel-Saturated Life	Characteristic 1A: Gospel-Centered Identity	Characteristic 1B: Gospel-Centered Actions
Quality #2 Connected to God	Characteristic 2A: Prayer Characteristic 2C: Incorporating Other Disciplines	Characteristic 2B: Connecting with God through His Word
Quality #3 Exhibiting the Fruit of the Spirit	Characteristic 3A: Sacrificial Living Characteristic 3C: Satisfied Living	Characteristic 3B: Gracious Living Characteristic 3D: Devoted Living
Quality #4 Understanding the Bible and Christian Theology	Characteristic 4A: Old Testament Literacy Characteristic 4C: Growth in Comprehension of Theological Knowledge	Characteristic 4B: New Testament Literacy Characteristic 4D: Studying the Word
Quality #5 Missional Living	Characteristic 5A: Understanding the Ministry of Jesus	Characteristic 5B: Incarnational Posture
Quality #6 Engaging Others toward Discipleship	Characteristic 6A: Helping Nonbelievers Come to Know the Lord	Characteristic 6B: Engaging Believers toward Discipleship
Quality #7 Community	Characteristic 7A: Local Congregation Commitment	Characteristic 7B: Deeper Christian Community
Quality #8 Fulfilling God's Call on Their Life	Characteristic 8A: Understanding of Gifts, Roles, and Calling	Characteristic 8B: Growing in Ministry Skill

The second step involved determining the questions that would help assess relative health within the stated qualities and characteristics. We began with more than two hundred potential questions. A new set of participants was asked to link questions with the qualities and characteristics. If questions were linked to multiple qualities, then the question was discarded. We took the remaining questions and inputted them into a survey for a new group of 150 participants to take about themselves, without asking others to take the assessment on their behalf. Dr. Wiens analyzed the results and eliminated questions that did not provide the statistical validity that is acceptable in the field.

Once the questions were narrowed and finalized, the closing step in the process was to get another group of one hundred participants to take the 360° version. In this case, the participant assessed their own discipleship and asked three to seven others to answer the questions on their behalf. This gave us the final statistical data to show that the assessment was both reliable and valid.

Reliability refers to an instrument's ability to produce the same results over multiple uses. Validity refers to an instrument's ability to measure what it says it is going to measure. Dr. Wiens and I are delighted that the resulting assessment meets and exceeds accepted standards in these areas. A full list of questions can be found in the sample report located on the Flourish website (www.flourishmovement.org).

HOW TO USE THE ASSESSMENT RESULTS

It is wonderful to have a tool that has gone through such a rigorous approval process. Once the survey is taken, however, we want to prayerfully discern how to interpret and apply the results. The process to apply the results differs from how one might apply the results of a blood test. A blood test will provide some hard numbers in areas such as cholesterol, triglycerides, and blood sugar. There is an established acceptable range for these numbers, and if numbers are higher or lower than the acceptable range, there are specific measures that should be taken to alter out-of-range numbers. For example, if triglycerides are too high, then the patient will want to reduce carbohydrate intake and increase fiber intake.

The simple discipleship assessment is not meant to be the only tool to diagnose the health of discipleship and then give a prescription; rather, the tool gives an individual a particular set of data to begin their prayerful exploration. For example, a newer disciple may have their lowest score in theological knowledge. While there will be a time when the disciple will want to grow in that particular area, this may not be the current place where God wants them to grow. They may explore their assessment with a friend, mentor, or small-group leader and see their prayer life (characteristic 2A) is also low and feel that this deeper connection to the Lord through prayer is the area in which they want to work.

It is also not uncommon to have the people who assess you give you higher scores than you give yourself. There are times, however, when this has happened for a person in all but one area. I have seen someone get higher ratings from observers in every area but Devoted Living. This quality looks at our ability to keep our commitments to God and one another. If a disciple assumes they are keeping their commitments and observers see that they don't, this may be an area for further exploration.

Another potential implication of observers giving consistently high ratings is that perhaps the disciple is putting on a false front to those around them. If there is a disproportionate result of higher scores in areas where people are assessing the inner life of the disciple, then perhaps the disciple wants to dig into this area more deeply.

Finally, the disciple will want to observe not only the scores that were given but also the comments that were made from the observers. Observers are asked where they have seen the disciple grow in recent months but also where they think the disciple should focus effort to grow in the coming months. These observers may or may not be familiar with the formal discipleship categories but will hopefully have an intuitive sense of an area of growth for the disciple.

This is all to say that the tool is not a definitive determiner of where a disciple should grow. It is, however, a great way to begin the process of determining where focused effort should be placed as the disciple grows in the image of Christ.

Resources to Aid in Discipleship Design Development

AS YOU DETERMINE AN area where you want to grow, the following is a beginning point for resources. This is not an exhaustive list; you are also encouraged to consult your pastor, local church, or denomination, or a network who may identify resources that align with your faith tradition.

OVERALL RESOURCES

- Design for Discipleship series by NavPress
- *Soul Keeping: Caring for the Most Important Part of You* by John Ortberg

QUALITY #1: Gospel-Saturated Life
- *The Prodigal God: Recovering the Heart of the Christian Faith* by Timothy Keller
- *Transforming Grace* by Jerry Bridges

QUALITY #2: Connected to God
- The 2:7 Series by NavPress
- *Spiritual Disciplines Handbook: Practices That Transform Us* by Adele Ahlberg Calhoun
- *Beginning the Walk: 18 Sessions on Jesus the Way, the Truth, and the Life* by NavPress

- *The Life You've Always Wanted: Spiritual Disciplines for Ordinary People* by John Ortberg

QUALITY #3: Exhibiting the Fruit of the Spirit
- *The Fruitful Life* by Jerry Bridges
- *Christlike: The Pursuit of Uncomplicated Obedience* by Bill Hull

QUALITY #4: Understanding the Bible & Christian Theology
- *Adventuring through the Bible: A Comprehensive Guide to the Entire Bible* by Ray C. Stedman

QUALITY #5: Missional Living
- *Sentness: Six Postures of Missional Christians* by Kim Hammond and Darren Cronshaw
- *Missional Essentials: A Guide for Experiencing God's Mission in Your Life* by Brad Briscoe and Lance Ford

QUALITY #6: Engaging Others toward Discipleship
- *Guardrails: Six Principles for a Multiplying Church* by Alan Briggs
- *42 Seconds: The Jesus Model for Everyday Interactions* by Carl Medearis
- *How to Ask Great Questions: Guide Discussion, Build Relationships, Deepen Faith* by Karen Lee-Thorp

QUALITY #7: Community
- *I Am a Church Member: Discovering the Attitude That Makes the Difference* by Thom S. Rainer
- *The Church as Movement: Starting and Sustaining Missional-Incarnational Communities* by JR Woodward and Dan White Jr.

QUALITY #8: Fulfilling God's Call on Their Life
- *Discover Your Spiritual Gifts: The Easy-to-Use Guide That Helps You Identify and Understand Your Unique God-Given Spiritual Gifts* by C. Peter Wagner
- APEST assessment by Alan Hirsch; see https://5qcentral.com/tests/

Sample Designs

Name: Jo Bloom (college sophomore)
Topic of Focus: Strengthening Biblical Knowledge
Goal: By May 31, I will

- possess a basic working knowledge of the names and order of the books and sections within the Bible; and

- become familiar with the content and flow of the book of Philippians.

ACTIVITIES TO ENGAGE WITH GOD (Spiritual)	ACTIVITIES TO ENGAGE WITH EXPERIENCE (Experiential)
• **Once a day**: Ask God to give me understanding and a command of the material I want to learn. • **Once a day**: Ask God to speak to me and guide me as I read Philippians and prepare a section to share with my peers.	• Prepare for and present on a section from Philippians to the youth group at my church. • Write out from memory the books of the Bible in order of appearance in the table of contents.
ACTIVITIES TO ENGAGE WITH OTHERS (Relational)	**ACTIVITIES TO ENGAGE WITH KNOWLEDGE AND TRUTH** (Instructional)
• **At least twice a week**: Converse with my parents about what I am reading in Philippians. • **Every other week**: Meet with Pastor Bob for an hour to discuss Philippians (usually Thursday at 2:00 p.m.). • Ask Mom, Dad, and Pastor Bob to pray daily for my growth in knowledge of the Bible and the book of Philippians.	• Regularly read through Philippians, making annotations and writing questions in a notebook. • Use reference books and online resources as needed. • Study, get familiar with, and memorize a chart of Bible books—using any variety of methods.

SAMPLE 2

Name: Shannon Creamer (forty-year-old wife and mother of two)
Topic of Focus: Discipline of Fasting
Goal: By March 27 (Easter),

- I will be practicing a regular discipline of fasting as a means to know and more freely love and serve Christ.

ACTIVITIES TO ENGAGE WITH GOD (Spiritual)	ACTIVITIES TO ENGAGE WITH EXPERIENCE (Experiential)
• **Daily**: Ask God to help me reach my goal. • **Daily**: Ask God to show me any obstacles preventing me from reaching my goal. • **Daily**: Ask God to speak and minister to me while I explore and establish the discipline of fasting.	• Guided by my notes from interviewing, praying, and reading, try a wake-up-until-dinner water fast and take notes or journal about my experience. • **By March 20**: Try a full-day fast (using what I have learned from resources and my partial-day fasting experience). • **By Lent**: Start some level of regular fasting.
ACTIVITIES TO ENGAGE WITH OTHERS (Relational)	ACTIVITIES TO ENGAGE WITH KNOWLEDGE AND TRUTH (Instructional)
• Ask three faithful friends to pray for me each day to reach my outcome. • **By January 15**: Invite a friend to explore fasting with me. • **By January 20**: Interview two Christians who regularly fast and take notes for use as I explore this practice.	• **By February 1**: Make a list of and examine all passages in the New Testament that relate to fasting. • **By February 1**: Read an article on fasting, taking notes for use as I explore this practice.

SAMPLE 3

Name: Steve Dooley (sixty-eight-year-old retired engineer)
Topic of Focus: Leading Small Group
Goal: By January 1,

- I will be prepared to begin leading a small group.

ACTIVITIES TO ENGAGE WITH GOD (Spiritual)	ACTIVITIES TO ENGAGE WITH EXPERIENCE (Experiential)
• **Daily**: Ask God for help and wisdom as I learn to lead a small group. • **Daily**: Ask God to give me insights about leading a group as I study His Word.	• Observe Bob and Sally's leadership of small group for one month. • Attend two other small groups (if appropriate). • **October**: Assist in leading a small group for the month. • **November**: Take primary leadership of a small group for the month.
ACTIVITIES TO ENGAGE WITH OTHERS (Relational)	**ACTIVITIES TO ENGAGE WITH KNOWLEDGE AND TRUTH** (Instructional)
• Ask my current small-group leaders, Bob and Sally, to pray for me as I seek to learn how to lead a small group. • Interview three small-group leaders about their experiences in leading a small group. • **Every two weeks**: Meet with Bob and Sally to give me guidance in leading a small group.	• **Daily**: Read the Gospels and journal about the characteristics of leadership as seen in Jesus. • **Weekly**: Read a chapter from *Leading Small Groups with Purpose*.

Notes

CHAPTER 1: The Essence of a Disciple

1. Merriam-Webster, s.v. "Shema," accessed April 29, 2018, https://www.merriam -webster.com/dictionary/Shema.
2. To learn more about the Shema and its meaning to the Israelites, see https://the bibleproject.com/blog/what-is-the-shema/.
3. Bible Study Tools: The NAS New Testament Greek Lexicon, s.v. "Kardia," accessed April 29, 2018, https://www.biblestudytools.com/lexicons/greek/nas/kardia.html.
4. For more information on the "neither cold nor hot" comment in Revelation 3:14-22, see: https://biblicalscholarship.wordpress.com/2012/10/19/commentary-on -revelation-314-22/.

CHAPTER 2: Jesus—the Great Disciple Maker

1. John Dear, *The Questions of Jesus: Challenging Ourselves to Discover Life's Great Answers* (New York: Image, 2004).

CHAPTER 4: Qualities of the Heart

1. Gary Chapman, *The 5 Love Languages: The Secret to Love That Lasts* (Chicago: Northfield Publishing, 2015).
2. Adele Ahlberg Calhoun, *Spiritual Disciplines Handbook: Practices That Transform Us*, rev. ed. (Downers Grove, IL: InterVarsity Press, 2015).
3. Bible Study Tools: The NAS New Testament Greek Lexicon, s.v. "Chrestotes," accessed May 10, 2018, https://www.biblestudytools.com/lexicons/greek/nas /chrestotes.html.
4. Gallup's StrengthsFinder assessment was designed by Don Clifton to help individuals discern their top strengths and stimulate personal and professional growth via the enhanced self-awareness resulting from this knowledge. For more information on this tool, visit https://www.gallupstrengthscenter.com/.

CHAPTER 6: Qualities of the Hand, Part 1

1. Don Everts and Doug Schaupp wrote the book *I Once Was Lost*, and in that book, they talk about the mini decisions that people make as they come to faith.

CHAPTER 8: Designing a Personal Plan for Discipleship

1. Learn more about Malcolm Webber and his paradigms for leader and disciple development at https://www.leadersource.org/about/models.php.
2. John Ortberg, "An Unhurried Life: The Practice of 'Slowing,'" chap. 5 in *The Life You've Always Wanted: Spiritual Disciplines for Ordinary People* (Grand Rapids, MI: Zondervan, 2015).

CHAPTER 10: Strategies and Environments for Discipleship

1. Alan Nelson and Gene Appel, *How to Change Your Church without Killing It*, with an introduction by Jim Mellado (Nashville, TN: W Publishing Group, 2000).
2. You can learn about *lectio divina* in Adele Ahlberg Calhoun's *Spiritual Disciplines Handbook*.

Take the Simple Discipleship Assessment!

PURCHASING THIS BOOK entitles you to one free assessment online. Taking the assessment will help you chart a course for your personal discipleship. You can access the assessment tool at the following page:

https://www.flourishmovement.org/assessments /discipleship-360-assessment/

Enter your exclusive code (found on the inside cover of this book) to take the assessment for free.

THE NAVIGATORS® STORY

T HANK YOU for picking up this NavPress book! I hope it has been a blessing to you.

NavPress is a ministry of The Navigators. The Navigators began in the 1930s, when a young California lumberyard worker named Dawson Trotman was impacted by basic discipleship principles and felt called to teach those principles to others. He saw this mission as an echo of 2 Timothy 2:2: "And the things you have heard me say in the presence of many witnesses entrust to reliable people who will also be qualified to teach others" (NIV).

In 1933, Trotman and his friends began discipling members of the US Navy. By the end of World War II, thousands of men on ships and bases around the world were learning the principles of spiritual multiplication by the intentional, person-to-person teaching of God's Word.

After World War II, The Navigators expanded its relational ministry to include college campuses; local churches; the Glen Eyrie Conference Center and Eagle Lake Camps in Colorado Springs, Colorado; and neighborhood and citywide initiatives across the country and around the world.

Today, with more than 2,600 US staff members—and local ministries in more than 100 countries—The Navigators continues the transformational process of making disciples who make more disciples, advancing the Kingdom of God in a world that desperately needs the hope and salvation of Jesus Christ and the encouragement to grow deeper in relationship with Him.

NavPress was created in 1975 to advance the calling of The Navigators by bringing biblically rooted and culturally relevant products to people who want to know and love Christ more deeply. In January 2014, NavPress entered an alliance with Tyndale House Publishers to strengthen and better position our rich content for the future. Through *THE MESSAGE* Bible and other resources, NavPress seeks to bring positive spiritual movement to people's lives.

If you're interested in learning more or becoming involved with The Navigators, go to www.navigators.org. For more discipleship content from The Navigators and NavPress authors, visit www.thedisciplemaker.org. May God bless you in your walk with Him!

Sincerely,

DON PAPE
VP/PUBLISHER, NavPress

www.navpress.com